THE EVERYTHING® GUIDE TO DAY TRADING

Dear Reader,

This book was written as a guide for people who are beginning to learn the art and science of day trading. While I have shied away from giving specific advice as to how to make your account grow with every trade, I have tried to include some of the subtleties of reading the economy, studying the markets, and structuring trades in general.

Day trading is a form of banking that goes way back to the beginning of organized markets. The most famous traders in history are the Italian bankers of the Renaissance. They traded in a market that was independent of the kings and monarchs of the time. The most profitable day trading the Italian bankers engaged in was with currencies and letters of credit. As the markets developed, other day trading opportunities came about in the Netherlands, Paris, and London.

It is my hope that you feel the same sense of connection to history as I do when you engage in the art, science, and mystery of day trading in the world's financial markets.

David Borman

Welcome to the EVERYTHING® Series!

These handy, accessible books give you all you need to tackle a difficult project, gain a new hobby, comprehend a fascinating topic, prepare for an exam, or even brush up on something you learned back in school but have since forgotten.

You can choose to read an *Everything*® book from cover to cover or just pick out the information you want from our four useful boxes: e-questions, e-facts, e-alerts, and e-ssentials.

We give you everything you need to know on the subject, but throw in a lot of fun stuff along the way, too.

We now have more than 400 *Everything*® books in print, spanning such wide-ranging categories as weddings, pregnancy, cooking, music instruction, foreign language, crafts, pets, New Age, and so much more. When you're done reading them all, you can finally say you know *Everything*®!

QUESTION

Answers to common questions

FACT

Important snippets of information

ALERT

Urgent warnings

ESSENTIAL

Quick handy tips

PUBLISHER Karen Cooper

DIRECTOR OF ACQUISITIONS AND INNOVATION Paula Munier

MANAGING EDITOR, EVERYTHING® SERIES Lisa Laing

COPY CHIEF Casey Ebert

ASSISTANT PRODUCTION EDITOR Jacob Erickson

ACQUISITIONS EDITOR Lisa Laing

ASSOCIATE DEVELOPMENT EDITOR Hillary Thompson

EDITORIAL ASSISTANT Ross Weisman

EVERYTHING® SERIES COVER DESIGNER Erin Alexander

LAYOUT DESIGNERS Colleen Cunningham, Elisabeth Lariviere, Ashley Vierra, Denise Wallace

Visit the entire Everything® series at *www.everything.com*

THE EVERYTHING® GUIDE TO DAY TRADING

All the tools, training, and techniques you need to succeed in day trading

David Borman

Avon, Massachusetts

This book is dedicated to my parents: my father, who told me to read every book I could, and my mother, who forced me to read every book I could.

Copyright © 2011 by F+W Media, Inc. All rights reserved.
This book, or parts thereof, may not be reproduced
in any form without permission from the publisher; exceptions
are made for brief excerpts used in published reviews.

An Everything® Series Book.
Everything® and everything.com® are registered trademarks of F+W Media, Inc.

Published by Adams Media, a division of F+W Media, Inc.
57 Littlefield Street, Avon, MA 02322 U.S.A.
www.adamsmedia.com

Contains material adapted and abridged from *The Everything® Investing Book, 3rd Edition* by Michele Cagan, copyright © 2009 by F+W Media, Inc., ISBN 10: 1-59869-829-X, ISBN 13: 978-1-59869-829-9.

ISBN 10: 1-4405-0621-3
ISBN 13: 978-1-4405-0621-5
eISBN 10: 1-4405-0622-1
eISBN 13: 978-1-4405-0622-2

Printed in the United States of America.

Library of Congress Cataloging-in-Publication Data
Borman, David.
The everything guide to day trading / David Borman.
p. cm.
Includes bibliographical references and index.
ISBN-13: 978-1-4405-0621-5 (alk. paper)
ISBN-10: 1-4405-0621-3
ISBN-13: 978-1-4405-0622-2 (ebook)
ISBN-10: 1-4405-0622-1 (ebook)
1. Day trading (Securities) 2. Electronic trading of securities. I. Title.
HG4515.95.B667 2011
332.64'2—dc22
2010040102

10 9 8 7 6 5 4 3 2 1

This publication is designed to provide accurate and authoritative information with regard to the subject matter covered. It is sold with the understanding that the publisher is not engaged in rendering legal, accounting, or other professional advice. If legal advice or other expert assistance is required, the services of a competent professional person should be sought.

—From a *Declaration of Principles* jointly adopted by a Committee of the American Bar Association and a Committee of Publishers and Associations

Many of the designations used by manufacturers and sellers to distinguish their products are claimed as trademarks. Where those designations appear in this book and Adams Media was aware of a trademark claim, the designations have been printed with initial capital letters.

This book is available at quantity discounts for bulk purchases.
For information, please call 1-800-289-0963.

Contents

Acknowledgments

I would like to say thank you to my editor, Lisa, who liked my ideas and gave me a chance. I would also like to thank all of the people (including my family) who had to listen for years to me babble on about this thing called "the stock market" and "day trading." I would also like to thank all of my past instructors and employers who gave me an opportunity and a place to learn about the markets from their experiences; and I would like to thank all of the other business writers—these are the ones who provided much of the material I have studied over the years. Finally, I would like to thank my brother, Teddy, who is the ultimate day trader.

The Top 10 Tips for Successful Day Trading

1. Learn to think of day trading as a business, and enter into each trade for the purpose of building up your cash account.
2. Learn how to use margin successfully—enough to leverage your cash balance but not too much to cause too much movement in your account.
3. Learn to use the 2% rule and pyramiding techniques to limit the risk in your account.
4. Learn to group your open positions into buckets of sectors that share the same market indicators.
5. Use both long-term and short-term timeframe technical charts to get a feel of where the market has been, where it is, and where it is going.
6. Know how to walk away from your trading desk after having a really good day in the markets.
7. Learn how to set up profitable trades when the world's stock markets are going strong, and how to reverse these trades when the markets are weak.
8. Have your entry points and exit points planned before you trade by using take-profit and stop-loss orders.
9. Look at your day trading profits on a per trade basis, all the while remembering that it is your monthly average that makes or breaks your day trading career.
10. Know that different sectors are hot at different times of the year. Develop your market knowledge of these sectors at the beginning of these seasons to help you spot day trading opportunities easier.

Introduction

ELECTRONIC SECURITIES DAY TRADING is actually a form of banking that can trace its roots back to the Renaissance. In those times, the bankers of Italy would discount banknotes and perform the much-needed function of exchanging currencies. This exchanging of currencies usually involved the issuing of a note of the needed currency that could be drawn against the issuing bank's foreign office. Information back then was hard to get, and the banks that could get advance notice of the exchange rate between the two currencies could make additional returns on currency deals.

Other advances in the concept of organized markets include the successful development of the stock exchanges in the Netherlands, Paris, and London. The markets were not without their flaws however, most notably marked by such events as Holland's Tulip Mania, the South Sea Bubble, and the stock market crash of 1929.

These events have been studied by many, and have resulted in many positive developments in trading on the exchanges. Further events in the evolution of day trading include the birth and proliferation of derivatives and the trading of futures on electronic platforms.

Another recent notable event was the end of the Bretton Woods system of currency pegging by mutual agreement. Its end in the early 1970s brought about an era of floating currencies. These floating currencies were mainly traded by merchant and investment banks until the widespread use of the Internet, which allowed the retail private market participant to day trade in her account.

It is true that day trading securities with a personal computer and the Internet is a relatively new idea. Personal computers are only a few decades old, and the Internet didn't become accessible to most everyone until the mid-to-late 1990s. It also took time for computer programmers to develop software that was sophisticated enough to handle the rigors of day trading in a fast-moving market.

Not only has technology developed to allow the private person to day trade, the brokerage business itself has changed. Gone are the days when the only place you could buy and sell securities was with a full-service broker. These full-service brokers are still around today, but there are even more choices available if you are looking for a no-frills, discount broker in which to do high volume trading. This has also been good for the retail day trader, as transaction costs have come way down, and are now in the range of under $10 per trade for equities at a deep-discount firm to over $100 per trade for equities at one of Wall Street's big full-service firms.

The adoption of a deep-discount firm may relieve the cost burden of frequent trading, but it will deprive you of a much-needed element to your day trading career: information. Information was a key element to the success of the banks of the Italian Renaissance. It was also a key element in the meteoric rise of one of the world's great banking families: the Rothschilds. Both banking groups sought out, collected, and used information to enhance the profitability of their endeavors. As you leave the world of the private bank and enter the world of the retail day trader using a deep-discount broker, there is an added need for guidance and information.

This book will give you the guidance and information you will need to successfully begin a career of day trading.

CHAPTER 1

Introduction to Markets and Trading

Mastering day trading takes knowledge. In order to thrive and do well with day trading you first have to know the functions of the markets, some of the commonly day traded financial products, and a bit about brokerage basics. Next you'll have to learn who some of the major players in the market are and where you fit in the mix. Lastly you'll have to know about some of the developments in modern trading and how to go global with your day trading business.

Day Trading and the Knowledge Factor

When someone mentions to you that they are a day trader, it may conjure images of someone sitting behind multiple computer screens showing blips of red and green information. You might also have visions of that person screaming buy and sell orders into a phone with a stock market television news station blaring in the background. You could also have thoughts of the huge quantities of money your friend must be making; or worse, when the market is going down, the huge sums of money your friend is losing.

You might be asking yourself, how do they do that? Or, how can they understand enough about those red and green blips to make a living at day trading in the market? You might go as far as to ask your day trader friend a question as to what stock he recommends. He might surprise you by answering that he only trades index futures, commodities, or things with a very exotic sounding names such as "FX."

Keep in mind your goals of what you would like to get out of learning how to day trade as you read this book. Relate the information and the lessons presented in the book to your short-, medium-, and long-term goals of being successful at day trading.

If you want, you too can learn to day trade. With a little practice, you could even build up your account to the point that you are making a steady profit with your day trading activities. Better yet, you could get to the point that you are drawing a salary against your account, and are ready to day trade full time. At this point you will be truly on your way toward having a successful day trading business.

Day trading can be very enjoyable, very exciting, and very profitable. Day trading is like no other business. There are very few requirements other than a computer, Internet access, and a place to trade. The key ingredient to a successful day trading business is knowledge. In fact, knowledge is often the most important element in day trading. The more you know about studying the economy, reading the markets, and spotting trends on the charts, the easier time you will have looking for set-ups, and getting into and out of trades profitably. It will take time to learn the day trading business, but you will find the time pays for itself in profitability and job satisfaction.

Functions of the Markets

Wherever markets have been, from the earliest money exchange houses to the most sophisticated electronic exchange, organized markets serve basic functions. **Price setting** is one of these functions, since the value of a security, whether a bushel of corn or a share of stock, is only worth what someone else will pay for it. Throughout history, the world's **bourses** (the world's meeting places and pits for trading securities, foreign exchange, or art and numismatics) have provided a place where buyers and sellers could meet and establish this price.

The markets also provide a forum for **price discovery**, or finding out the going rate of an item that is to be transacted. Prices are based upon what others have paid for the same item in previous exchanges; this price discovery is a form of **asset valuation**. Asset valuation serves as a method of determining the value of property or claims on property without the actual sale of the property. To arrive at an effective valuation, the two pieces of property must be similar in nature, quality, and quantity.

Don't be fooled! The actual reason the equities markets such as the New York Stock Exchange exist is to have a place where companies can come to market and raise money for their businesses. This is referred to as the **primary market.** Once a stock is sold for the first time, it then enters what is called the **secondary market.**

This similarity of nature, quality, and quantity is evident in the futures market and where each contract is 100 percent interchangeable with a contract of the same product throughout the world. A contract for 100 ounces of gold is the same as 100 ounces of .999 fine gold throughout the world. The same is for a corn contract, a wheat contract, or a copper contract. This uniformity is very prevalent in organized exchanges; i.e., your share of IBM is the same as someone else's share of IBM.

Another function of the markets is to provide an opportunity for traders to profit from **arbitrage**. Arbitrage is the act of simultaneously buying and selling the same security on different markets in order to profit from the momentarily and fleeting difference in price. With arbitrage, you short the higher priced security and go long the lower price security, and close out both orders at a profit when the prices of the two converge at an equal price. In theory, arbitrage does not exist: All markets that are fully functioning have equal pricing, and all market facts are known by all participants. In reality, opportunities to make money on the price differences of securities between markets do exist, however fleeting. Other functions include giving the world's companies an arena to raise capital for the continuation of their lines of work or for expansion. This capital-raising often means a company's issuing of new stock or new **tranches**, or large orders to be placed with institutional investors. Tranches are often bundled together to have the same financial characteristics, and are often sold in units of $1 million or more per order. The money raised by issuing stock is put directly into the **coffers**, or the cash accounts of the issuing company, and in exchange for money, the buyers of the stock receive an ownership stake in the company. The last function of the world's financial market includes offering the individual an opportunity for investing and profiting from the short-term fluctuations in price, commonly referred to as day trading.

Commonly Traded Products

Trading in the foreign exchange market goes back to the 1300s and 1400s when people would travel between countries and bring back the gold and silver coins of foreign lands. These people were unable to use the different countries' coinage in their own countries, as the shopkeepers and merchants in the home countries were unfamiliar with the weight and fineness of the gold and silver content.

The process of measuring, weighing, and testing for fineness is an ancient process, and often led to the money changer exchanging the foreign coinage for a local coinage at a discount to the actual gold or silver weight and fineness of the coin. The process was carried further throughout history to the Florentine bankers of the Renaissance discounting bank notes, up to the adoption of the Euro as the common currency of many European nations. **Foreign exchange trading** is done in the spot market, in the futures market, and with custom-made, interbank derivatives such as forwards and swaps. A **forward** is much like a future, where a contract is signed to buy a financial asset in the future at a set price, but in the case of forwards, the contract is custom made between the parties and is not freely tradable on an exchange. In the case of **swaps**, a custom made contract is entered into with the obligation of both parties to trade securities (usually FX) at the beginning of the contract and return like securities back to the original owners at the end of the term by "re-swapping" the exact or like securities. Swaps and forwards are done off of the exchange, are for very large and irregular amounts, and are usually arranged between the world's largest banking institutions and hedge funds.

The currency markets are by far the largest market in the world with over $3 trillion traded daily. Compare that to the size of the world's equity markets, which are valued at around $30 trillion in total. The size of the world derivative market is difficult to determine due to the pricing system inherent to derivatives.

The equity markets are a source of another set of frequently traded products, stocks, and **exchange traded funds (ETFs)**.

Stocks are an ownership share of a company, and the stock market can trace its roots back to the Dutch East India Company in 1602. The Dutch East India Company was formed by Dutch businessmen; they sold shares in their company that were fully negotiable. In other words, the shares could be traded on the exchanges in Amsterdam.

Following this, there was the development of the joint-stock company in London in the late 1600s. Today, stocks are traded in most every major financial center in the world. ETFs are a relatively new concept, with the diversification qualities of **mutual funds** and the inter-day tradability of stocks. These ETFs are much like a basket of securities that trade as one security. They are especially useful for trading baskets of stocks and indexes that would not be otherwise accessible to the average trader. This would include access to foreign stock indexes and emerging market indexes.

The trading of **commodities** goes hand in hand with the trading of **futures**. Futures trading involves the trading of an electronic form of a written contract to buy or sell an underlying product at a set price at a set time in the future. They were used in the Renaissance to ensure merchants that profits would be made on an incoming shipment of goods before the shipment would arrive. Both parties agreed on the selling price, and a contract would be signed that would commit the merchant to sell the product to the holder of the contract at that price when the shipment arrived. In this process, the merchant could arrive at a price that would insure the profitability of the shipment of goods, and the holder of the contract could lock in the cost of the goods used as raw materials in his product. In the sixteenth century, contracts were made on the future catches of herring that fishermen had not yet caught. These too served to lock in the profits of the fishermen and lock in the expenses of the buyers who needed the herring. Fast-forward to the modern day—this leaves you with the modern exchanges where commodities such as copper, gold, wheat, and coffee are traded in standardized and uniform contract sizes. There has even been the advent of equities index futures and futures whose values are directly tied to the weather.

IPOs and Brokerage Basics

When a company first wants to raise money in the market it will go to an investment bank and employ the investment bank to organize an **initial public** offering, or **IPO**. IPOs are usually the first attempt by a successful privately held company to raise cash for expansion by selling shares of itself to institutional investors and the public.

A valuation of the company is made, and the number of pieces of the company will be offered as well as an initial offering price. After much number crunching and legal work, the investment bank will go on a "road show" to promote and test the waters of public interest in the company. Sometimes the investment bank will take presale orders for blocks of shares for its best customers, usually institutional investors and hedge funds.

When the shares are first offered to the public, the company is in the process of **going public**. This going public is the dream of many business owners across the globe, as the cash that can be raised by such an IPO can be dramatic, and of course, a company's original owners will retain a certain number of shares for themselves. If they are not already millionaires, many business owners become millionaires overnight with the introduction of an IPO.

Don't bet on getting into any Initial Public Offering at the beginning. You can rest assured that the investment banks keep the best IPOs for their best clients. Any IPO that would be available to a normal retail customer would most likely not be worth getting into in the first place.

In order to buy a security you would need to have an account with a brokerage firm. There are two types of brokerage firms: the **full-service firm** and the **discount firm**. Opening an account with a full-service firm will give you access to a licensed representative who is trained in securities selection and the setting up of trades. She can offer you advice as to how the economy affects your trading as well as steer you into trades that offer the best profit potential. Most full-service firms allow you to trade almost all classes of securities from equities to futures to foreign exchange, and can also offer competitive interest rates on the unused cash portion of your portfolio.

Another advantage to full-service firms is the access to proprietary research reports on every asset class imaginable, some even going as far as to offer entry and exit points for profitable trading. Access to the long-term economic reports that are issued by the broker can also be a key element in successful day trading.

The second type of brokerage firm is the discount firm. Discount firms offer the same back office, order entry, and market access as a full-service firm. The only difference is that you will not have a representative to speak with, and most likely the discount firm will not offer its own research, but will rely on outside sources for this critical information instead.

The Players

There are several main players in the world of trading. In the first group are the investment banks and the hedge funds. While **investment banks** offer IPO services, corporate finance, and brokerage accounts, some trade on their own accounts and with their own money. This type of trading is called **proprietary trading**, and can offer an investment bank a healthy return on the capital involved, often adding dramatically to its bottom line. In fact, there are times when the markets are doing exceedingly well that an investment bank will shrink the amount of resources that it is investing in its traditional lines of work, and invest heavily in proprietary trading. This shifting of resources from one profit center to another is quite common with the world's major banks, as is the shifting back into more fee-based and conservative lines of work, such as advising, when the market is performing poorly.

FACT

There are many types of hedge funds in the investment universe. In fact a hedge fund is only limited in its investment style by the imagination of its fund manager. Some funds have the goal of stability at the cost of returns, and there are others who have high returns as the goal of the fund.

The other members of this large group are the **hedge funds**. Hedge fund managers are often very entrepreneurial and share in their funds' profits. The fees that a typical fund manager can expect to receive are 2 percent of the gross amount managed annually and 20 percent of the total profits, paid out quarterly. These large percentages offer a very strong incentive for a hedge fund manager to know his market, and trade for maximum profit. They often have a large percentage of their own assets invested in the fund, and are sometimes the hedge fund's major shareholder.

Sophisticated computer programs and mathematics are a hallmark of these funds. Other common threads in the hedge fund world include advanced degrees from Ivy League institutions and a high degree of secrecy. Because hedge funds lay outside the normal investment arena, they are somewhat unregulated, and there are different legal requirements to manage a hedge fund than the management of other investments such as mutual funds.

The other main players are central governments and their central banks. These banks can and often do intervene in the currency markets to stabilize or change the value of their home currency. These are the major players in the foreign exchange world. Because of this, when a major central bank is intervening in the market, the market will move. This is because the entire force of those governments' financial reserves can be called into play to change the direction of a home currency. When a central bank makes a move in the market, it will usually be reported in its public statements.

Other market participants include mutual funds and other institutions. Mutual funds and institutions such as **endowments** and **pension funds** buy and sell large amounts of securities as a whole, and account for much of the trading volume of the exchanges.

Lastly, there is the **independent investor and trader**. An independent investor usually has a buy and hold strategy of selecting securities and holding them for the long term. Independent traders are the group of people who day trade in their privately held accounts with their private money. They are the only ones to share in the profits derived from day trading.

Modern Trading and Going Global

The invention and proliferation of the Internet brought the world of online trading to the average person. Before this, a trader would place a call to his or her broker and place a buy or sell order. Now, a day trader can open up an Internet connection virtually anywhere in the world and have access to her account, check her balance, and monitor her positions. Some of the newest technology allows access to an account with a truly portable, mobile device.

This introduction of online trading was coupled with the deep-discount broker to give birth to the modern day trader. Technology has gotten better and cheaper, and competition in the brokerage world has lowered transaction costs. The combined effect is to make the conditions required for a profitable day trading business. There have been advances in the security of online accounts, including encryption, passwords, and key codes. In the beginning, many people had concerns with doing business on the Internet. This is not a concern as much anymore.

The hours that the markets are open have also changed from the early morning to the early afternoon to after-hours trading to a truly twenty-four-hour market in some sectors. Not only have some sectors gone with twenty-four-hour trading, with the introduction of the Internet, there is greater access to the international markets, allowing for a truly global marketplace.

Don't be put off by the thought of opening up an offshore account. Contrary to recent news, they are not illegal. What is illegal is when a U.S.-based holder of an offshore account does not report to the IRS the fact that the offshore account is held by the tax filer.

You can invest in foreign stocks, foreign indexes, and the indexes of developing parts of the world. This global investing can be done with an ETF in a U.S.-based brokerage firm, or for a truly global experience, you could open up an account at one of the international firms. These international firms are known as **offshore brokers**. These offshore brokers are in some ways easier to set up, but are in some ways a bit more difficult to get money into and out of.

Of course, if you open up an offshore account at one of the many investment houses available, you would have to fill out a special tax form and file it with the U.S. IRS, indicating that you are the owner of an account that is held outside of the United States and its territories. Not to worry, though, as the form is easy to fill out, and can easily be handled by a CPA or tax attorney.

Popular jurisdictions for offshore accounts include Luxembourg, Switzerland, Austria, Cyprus, and the Isle of Man. These accounts would offer you access to the markets and investment products that would be unavailable with a U.S.-based account.

CHAPTER 2

What Is Day Trading?

As you consider a day trading career and lifestyle, you should first learn how day trading differs from investing. It would also help if you had a good grasp of some basic economic, banking, and day trading terms as well as a general knowledge of the differences in trading methods. Finally, you will see how a typical day trader spends a good day, as well as how a bad trading day might unfold. Overall, this view will help you determine if you might enjoy and succeed at day trading.

Day Trading Defined

In order to consider if you would like to be a day trader, you will first have to know what day trading is, and what it means to be day trading the markets as opposed to investing in the markets.

Investing

In order to get a good grasp on day trading the markets it will help to look at its exact opposite: investing in the markets. Investing in the markets usually involves some sort of thought as to your entire overall financial present and future. For example, you might determine that you are thirty-five years old, have a long time left on a mortgage, a baby on the way, and three months emergency money stashed away in a savings account. With planning, you determine that you will need to save $500–$650 a month put away in a brokerage account and invested at a growth rate of 8 percent to reach your goal of retiring early and sailing around the world on a catamaran. With analysis, it is possible to choose the proper mix (diversification) of stocks, bonds, and mutual funds that combined will produce the required amount of return for your risk level. With this predetermined plan of where to invest, you would most likely invest enough with each paycheck to add up to the dollar amount needed to reach your goals. You would use the **dollar cost averaging** method of buying at regular intervals, at high points of the market and at low points of the market.

The method of dollar cost averaging in the day trading world is called pyramiding (or the **pyramid method**). Pyramiding is entering and exiting trades with three equal dollar amounts in order to smooth your average position cost and selling price. This buying and selling method is a form of safe position management.

This dollar cost averaging technique would lead to the second method commonly used in investing: **buy and hold**. The buy and hold philosophy is one of buying a security, whether it be a stock, bond, or mutual fund, and holding it for the long term, usually five to seven years or longer. Since five to seven years is usually considered the average length of a market cycle, the theory is that you would capture the full benefits of the upward movement in the market within this time. At the end of the market cycle, you would sell, and rotate the sales proceeds into the opposite investment vehicle to capture its gains for that product's full investment cycle. As bonds usually do well when stocks are doing poorly, you could start in a bond fund, ride it to the top of its value (the end of the market cycle), sell, and switch to the opposite, a stock mutual fund.

Day Trading Is Really Micro Investing

The theories behind proper and profitable investing can be applied to day trading. You would first look at the amount of money you have in your trading account, and how much margin you have available. You would then determine where you would like to be in the future. For example, you determine that you would like to make enough money day trading this month to pay for your expenses, the car payment, and the condo payment. You would add up how much you would need in dollar amounts and divide it by four to make weekly goals.

Let's say that the condo payment, car, and expenses add up to $1,600. Divided by four, you realize that your profit goal is $400 per week, and divided further, your goal is $80 per trading day. You would basically make this your ultra-short-term investing goal, i.e., micro investing. You would use your brokerage account and product diversification to make a series of purchases to build positions using the same philosophy as investing's dollar cost averaging. You would also use the **philosophy of buy and hold**, but with that of a day trader's perspective of buying and holding for minutes and hours, and at the most a few days (the average length of a market's ultra-short-term movements in one direction). Using the same theories of investing, such as goal-orientated investing (pay bills), risk-reward (diversification across and within sectors), dollar cost averaging (building positions during the day), and buy and hold (minutes, hours, or days), you would think of day trading as micro investing your way to a higher net worth.

Trading Terminology

To begin your day trading career, there are a few words that you should be familiar with. These terms are used throughout the day trading world, and a firm understanding of them will help you read fundamental analysis reports and technical charts, as well as study the financial markets, economics, and day trading. Although this will serve as the extreme basics of a vocabulary list, your knowledge of the terms associated with the markets and day trading will grow naturally as you gain experience in day trading.

▼ ECONOMIC AND BANKING TERMS

Advancing Market	An average upswing in market prices across an entire sector
Analyst	An investment professional who makes comments and predictions about a company, industry sector, or the entire economy
Appreciation	The growth of the value of a security over time
Auction Market	Trading securities through brokers and dealers to get the best prices for buyers and sellers
Balance Sheet	The financial accounting of a company's assets, debts, and equity. Is frequently used as one of the tools to assess a company's financial health
Bear Market	A steady, long-term downward trend in a market or sector
Beta	A mathematical measurement of risk in relation to the entire overall market with a beta of one being equal to the market's risk. For example, a stock might have a beta of 1.5 would have 150% the risk of the overall market, and a stock with 0.25 beta would have 25% the risk of the overall market
Bull Market	A long-term upward trend in a market or sector
Central Bank	A government established bank that issues currency, holds reserves of other banks, and administers policy
Economic Report	Statements issued through government entities and research departments to make comments on the economic health of a business sector, geographic region, or entire country
Fundamental Analysis	The use of a company's financial statements to predict future cash flows and stock price
Technical Analysis	The study of charts to predict the future price of a security or overall market
Market Indicator	Factors that are used to accurately predict the direction of markets

After you learn the economic and banking terms, the next terms to learn are the ones directly related to day trading:

▼ **DAY TRADING TERMS**

Going Long	A term used to state you have a trade that is set up to make money when the security or sector is moving upward
Margin	A form of credit in a brokerage account used to purchase securities
Net Profit on a Trade	The amount realized from a transaction, minus the transaction fees, minus the price of entry, leaving the overall profit on the trade
Order Entry	The method that an online trading terminal uses to actually purchase or sell a security
Shorting	A term used to state you have a trade that is set up to make money when the security or sector is moving downward
Unrealized Profit or Loss	The profit or loss that you would make on a trade if you closed the trade at that exact moment

Additional economic, banking, and day trading terminology knowledge can be developed through the study of your brokerage firm's research reports and by reading the daily news wire services.

Most brokerage firms offer an "education" section that includes complete lists of the thousands of words used in the investment, banking, and day trading world. Other sources of complete terminology lists include investment and banking dictionaries as well as investment dictionaries that are electronically embedded directly into some trading software.

Day Trading versus Position Trading versus Hybrid Methods

Whether buying stock and selling it when it goes up, or selling stock and replacing it when it goes down, the idea of trading remains the same: The money you make is the price difference at which you are in and out of the trade. However, there are different strategies to trading, and one of the differences is the length that you, as the trader, are holding the stock, exchange traded funds (ETF), or commodity. This is called the **time in the trade**.

Day Trading

In day trading there are two basic types of trading styles, with the first being day trading in its purest form. A trader will ride the movement of the stock market, futures market, or foreign exchange market with very little regard as to where the medium- and long-term trends are heading. She will rely on **technical analysis** (a system of reading charts off a computer screen) in an attempt to spot short- and very short-term movements in the sector being traded.

Sometimes the trader will trade only in the beginning of the trading day or only at the end of the trading day. These are usually the times of the heaviest market activity as traders and investors all over the world are actively managing their positions. The beginning of the day marks the time at which traders are reacting to news that happened overnight, and the end of the day is the time that market participants are making adjustments to their portfolios in a reaction to the early part of the day.

If you were a pure day trader you would begin the day with your account invested in 100 percent cash. You wouldn't have anything in your accounts other than cash and your **available margin**, which is a form of a credit card for buying stock or other tradable sector. You would buy and sell in your account all day or all night, moving in and out of many, many trades during your work day. You would add to your account with gains and subtract to your account with losses. Before you ended your day, after just a few hours or after the closing bell, you would close out all of your positions and return to 100 percent cash. You would start the next day with cash again, with more or less than the preceding day according to your profits or losses.

Position Trading

The second method of trading that works well is **position trading**. With this method, you accumulate more and more of a particular trade over time. To start, pre-determine your trades by doing economic, accounting, financial, and technical chart research. Consult other traders to see what they are thinking. You might speak with your full-service broker to see what his investment bank's research department thinks. Then, use computer charts showing hourly and daily price movements, not five- and thirty-second price movements. Make a case for the trade and start building it:

this is your **position**. As the trade sells off and moves lower, you buy more, using the adage **buy on the dips**. In the end, sell off your position at the highest possible range of its long-term movement.

Hybrid Methods

A combination of both pure day trading and position trading can lead to very profitable trading situations. For example, you could determine that Norway is in very good economic shape. Your research shows that Norway is running a current account surplus due to the fact that its North Sea oil production is being sold worldwide. You know that a current account surplus means that the country has more exports than imports, and intakes more foreign money than it pays out. Surpluses usually make a country's currency stronger over time due to economic factors and interest rates. Its main trading partners include the nations of continental Europe, who use the euro (EUR) as their common currency. You also learn from research that Europe is experiencing a slowing economy and its central bank in Brussels, Belgium, will most likely lower the euro's interest rates. You conclude that due to all these factors, the krone (NOK) will appreciate against the euro. With this in mind, you begin to accumulate a short position in EUR/NOK, meaning you will make money as the NOK gets stronger.

Carry trades (going with long, high-yielding currencies versus low-yielding currencies) can have huge one-way positions that are built up worldwide, with each additional trade stretching the carry trade further and further until it reaches a breaking point. When this happens, traders will all try to unravel their trades at once, with a rapid devaluing of the long currency.

The other parts of your total available trading cash are used to ride the ups and downs of the S&P 500 by trading in and out of an ETF. An ETF acts like an artificial grouping of many stocks all bundled together in one tradable share. Sometimes during the day you are trading a 1:1 representation of the S&P 500 index, meaning that each percentage move of the overall index is matched with a percentage move in the ETF. During volatile, rapid ups and downs, you might switch to a 2:1 or 3:1 geared ETF.

These ETFs would capture the percentage movements in the S&P 500 index with a factor of 2 or 4. In other words, if the overall stock market went through turmoil and fell 3, 4, or 5 percentage points and reversed itself at the end of the day, you would capture the percentage movements to the upside by two or three times as much. This would mean gains from 6 percent to 15 percent from the market's bottom to top ride. Again, you would move out of all positions in this part of your account by the end of the day.

While the days go by and you are in and out of trades by the end of the market's close, your short-medium trade in EUR/NOK is creeping higher and higher with each day. You have committed a small part of your overall trading capital, but you have used a very large amount of margin, say 100:1 or 200:1. This means for every dollar of cash you committed to the trade you bought 100 or 200 dollars worth of currency. You close out the trade after six weeks of holding it, as the NOK went up 3 percent against the euro. Your profit is 300 percent to 600 percent of the amount of capital you put into the trade. After this one big money-making trade, you might decide to close out of all of your ETF trades and take the rest of the week off.

The Benefits and Downsides of Day Trading

There are good and bad aspects to every career. In the course of business, you, as a professional day trader, will experience the best and the worst of the issues that people experience in normal nine-to-five, forty-hour-a-week jobs.

Benefits of Day Trading

One of the benefits to a day trading career is the large amount of money that can be made during the peak seasons of the trading year. While the market is open year round, during different times of the year, different sectors are very popular to trade. Along with this popularity comes the opportunity for a day trader to make an income that far exceeds what he could make working at a regular job. The market can make you rich very quickly, and there are stories of professional day traders closing up shop around the holidays and flying the whole extended family out to Aspen for a week-long skiing trip.

A second benefit to day trading is the self-directed working schedule. You, as the professional day trader, are able to take any day off that you would like. If you feel as though you have made enough profit for the week and it is Thursday morning at 10 A.M., you can close out of all of your positions and take a four-day weekend. You can also trade part-time while you are working a regular job. You could supplement your income day trading or "night trading" one of the market sectors that are open twenty-four hours a day. After spending the day working in an office, construction site, school, or as a full-time parent, you could log into your trading account and day trade into the evening.

Downfalls of Day Trading

While there are bad aspects of day trading, many of these can be prevented with good money management, good trade-size management, increased knowledge of the markets, and a healthy support group. For instance, day trading by nature requires money, or capital, to make a trade. Granted, some day trading accounts allow you to use **margin**, (a form of a revolving credit card for buying stocks, currencies, or futures), but you will need to have some cash in your account to begin day trading. If you are day trading part-time, a small amount of money will work. To day trade as a full-time career, and to make a living at it, you will need enough cash to make bigger trades—to be able to make enough **weekly average profit** to make bi-weekly or monthly cash withdrawals from the account. These withdrawals are to be made to cover your expenses related to trading and to give yourself a livable salary.

It is almost a paradox: To make a living at day trading, you have to have enough money in your account to the point that you almost do not need to rely on day trading for profit!

Secondly, the nature of your living being tied to the market can lead to wild swings in your fortunes, both good and bad. You could have a great day, week, or month, and then begin to slowly suffer from typical trader's curses: changing strategies, markets, margin amounts, or otherwise venturing into riskier and riskier trades. It is easy to develop a taste for risk, and this can lead to a not-so-well placed trade. A trade such as this could go bad. If it does, the movement from this one or this series of trades can lead to losses. Sometimes the losses are large enough to wipe out your previous gains, which can effectively bring your account back to breakeven, or worse.

While you will naturally be looking at your profit/loss sheet on an hourly and daily basis, you should keep the longer term in perspective. For example, the proprietary trading desks of investment banks report their earnings on a per-quarter basis. Additionally, the investment bank's traders are paid salaries with performance-based bonuses awarded at the end of the year.

The last problem with day trading is the fact that often times you spend time alone, day trading the markets in your office or home, day after day. The television and radio become your only co-workers, keeping you company during good days and bad. You can forget how much you enjoy getting the input of others on a trading idea, to share a big profit, or to just talk it though after a big loss. You can best manage this aspect of the independent day trader lifestyle with both professional and personal friends, support groups, and family.

A Typical Good Trading Day

You might be wondering what a typical day is for a day trader. First, you have to understand that there are two types of trading days: the profitable trading days and the losing days. With skill and good money and margin management, a trader will spend most days like the following.

In this example of a good trading day, you as the day trader are trading in the foreign exchange markets. You begin your work week on Sunday evening, as the markets open. Scanning the list of upcoming economic reports, you discover that the Swiss National Bank will be making an announcement on Thursday.

The report will be on the Swiss economy's unemployment and inflation figures. Since you have been watching the development of the Swiss franc

(CHF) for some time, you are aware that the Swiss National Bank, or SNB, has been concerned with the fact that the franc has been appreciating in value against the euro.

After checking your broker's research on the currency pair and scanning over your charts, you decide to place an automated **stop**, where the trading platform will automatically sell Swiss francs against euros when it reaches a certain point in the next few days. Certain you will make money on this trade, you use 200:1 leverage and commit a large amount of your account.

By now the foreign exchange desks in Asia are in full swing, and your trading platform is lighting up with flickers of red and green, signaling the up and down movement of the different currency pairs. Since your favorite actress is going to be starring in a movie on television in a few minutes, you decide to spend the night watching the movie and placing small, easy trades.

Flipping from chart to chart, you use good money management and use a small amount of your margin available. Because your plan is to be in and out of a trade within five minutes, you use a short timeframe chart and ignore the big multiple hour and day charts. You sit there all night long on the couch watching the movie, and capture profits by trading the euro (EUR), yen (JPY), New Zealand dollar (NZD), and Swedish krona (SEK). With up to six different trades going on the screen, you casually pay attention and close out each trade as it slowly creeps into the profit zone.

Some foreign exchange traders use the trading platform provided by their brokers to program buy and sell orders in the evening. Using their market knowledge of entry and exit points, they predetermine their profits for each trade. Before they go to work in the morning, they check their accounts to find the orders executed, locking their profits while they slept.

It's now 2 A.M. and the European traders are getting into the markets. You've sat through three movies and are about to start your fourth. You check your profits for the night, and you see that you've made more money than you would have spending an eight-hour day at a regular job, all without the commute. Deciding to call it a good night, you close out your remaining trades and go to bed. In a few hours the kids will be waking up and you'd like to drive them to school.

A Typical Bad Trading Day

While most of your days would be spent like the ones above, there is the potential for a bad day to happen. Keep in mind that much of what happens in the narrative below can be prevented with money management, position size, and market knowledge.

Monday and Tuesday were such good days in the foreign exchange market that you decided to take Wednesday off and go to the beach. While at the beach you watched the power boats cruise by and the swimmers in the water. You generally enjoyed yourself in the sunshine away from your computer and the markets. In the evening you went to a pizza place with some friends from your old job, where they envied the fact that you were doing so well being on your own, and in their minds, "not working." You went home that night feeling good about your new career, and the fact that you would not have to ride the train to work tomorrow. The next morning thoughts of your friends hurrying to work are mixed with thoughts of glee. You get the kids off to school and settle in for "not working" by day trading in the foreign exchange market. Grabbing another cup of coffee, you flip on the news. The anchor on CNBC is talking about exchange rates in Europe, something about the Swiss franc.

With just a little bit of the jitters, you fire up your computer to view your positions. Baffled, you look at a chart of the EUR/CHF pair. It doesn't look right. There are a lot of flickers from red to green all over the screen, and you can see the market is in its heaviest trading hours, when the European markets overlap with the U.S. markets. Then you see it. The stop order you placed on Sunday was filled automatically sometime since you last looked at your account. The green point on the EUR/CHF chart shows the exact time the automated trading platform filled your order. It shows Thursday 3 A.M. central time, or 10 A.M. Zurich time.

You see on the chart that your order was filled just moments before the Swiss National Bank's announcement, when the franc got weaker by heavy speculative selling. The problem, though, is that the chart shows that the franc got weaker for about five minutes and then reversed its direction and got stronger. In fact, the chart shows the franc getting stronger and stronger ever since the SNB's announcement.

It is important to keep track of the dates when important economic announcements will be made. You can go to the websites of the reserve banks of the world's major countries and economies to get an overview of when announcements will be made and when economic reports will be released.

You quickly look at the part of the screen that shows your unrealized profit. You're at a loss and it looks bad. "What did the SNB say?" you ask yourself as you scan the Internet news feeds. The official statement from Zurich is that " . . . the SNB is okay with a stronger franc and has no intentions on any official intervention in the future." You realize you called it wrong. Knowing that the franc will never weaken in the short term with such an official statement, you look at how bad the damages are. All the profits from Monday and Tuesday have been wiped out. Your account is back to the balance you had on Sunday night. You take a deep breath and face the facts: There is nothing you can do now to correct the trade, and you close out your position at a big loss. Looking at the bright side, you think to yourself, "I'm still up for the week." You shut down the computer and turn off the news. Taking the rest of the day off, you go to the mall for some retail therapy.

CHAPTER 3

Is Day Trading for You?

Now that you know a little about what day trading is and how day traders spend their days, you can start to decide if day trading is for you. There are emotional considerations, time commitments, your availability of funds, and of course the question of if you can work alone. There is also the question of your other responsibilities, if you have a backup plan, and what to do when the day trading world is especially difficult to navigate.

Emotions and Temperament

The first things you should consider are the emotions of the job. All jobs come with a certain emotional commitment to perform the job effectively. The effect of having your income tied to the uncontrolled ups and downs of the market can lead to a form of emotional mania and depression. When you are trading the market and have a profitable day, you can be floating in a euphoric-like place where nothing can affect you. Certainly this is a very positive emotion to experience, but as the markets reverse and your trading account shows losses, you could experience the opposite. Your emotions at these times could be just as low as the market is. This unmanaged emotional up and down of the market can become a thrill ride in itself, where you are always looking for the next wild swing of feelings. With this in mind, it is important to learn how to stand back and look at trading as a job and your trading account as your tools.

A mechanic would be excited when a customer brought in a Ferrari to be worked on, but he would engage the tune-up, carburetor adjustment, and engine rebuild with a cool, professional "separateness" apart from his love of Italian cars. He would not abuse his wrenches or gauges in such a way as to diminish their value or harm them in any way. This is a good way to start to think about trading and your trading account. You will be "working on" very expensive, exotic things while using your precious tools of the trade, i.e., you will trade a particular sector using your precious trading account.

Day trading is like being a Stone-Age hunter. You will use the most basic of tools, cash, and margin (rocks and spears), to go after game. You can go after the easy, smaller animals more often (with less risk), or you could go after larger animals with more meat less often (but with increased risk).

This idea of trading as a professional or treating trading like a business is one of the key elements to a successful long-term day trading career. Your emotions can be tied to every trade before it is made. You can learn to use a cool head to plan **entry points** (the point at which you make your initial purchase of a stock, commodity, or currency), as well as using calm, calculated feelings to execute an exit from a trade to capture profits. There are many stories of day traders feeling elated with their **unrealized gains** on a trade (unrealized means the profits are still "on paper" and not yet in the day trader's account, as the trade has not been closed out yet) and not able to exit the trade in hopes of more gains. With these stories the trade turns bad, and the profits are lost. These traders go on to tell stories of how they "should have taken the profits," and "what was I thinking?" If you can learn how to manage your emotions of trading, you can really be on your way to making money on good trading days and keeping your money on bad trading days. In day trading, good emotion management is important for good money management.

Time Commitment

The second thing to consider before you begin your day trading career is if you can make the time commitment. Depending on where you are with your personal overall market knowledge, it can take anywhere from one month to several seasons to get enough general knowledge to begin successfully trading. You have to commit yourself to a somewhat structured study period for a few weeks at the minimum to get acquainted with the markets by reading books and magazines designed for independent day traders, as well as skimming through the daily business newspapers such as the *Wall Street Journal* and the *Financial Times*. Often, people want to start placing trades and making profits immediately.

If you would like to be as successful as possible, it would be best if you took your time to learn the markets before committing any amount of money. There are stories of people opening an account online in a matter of minutes, depositing money, and hurrying to trade. There are also stories of day traders placing trades in fresh accounts when they aren't even sure how to use the trade input screens. They then made trades in the wrong direction and for the wrong amount. Such disasters can be avoided by taking your time while opening an account, learning how to operate it, and learning about what you would like to trade.

Trading also takes time once you are in full swing, as it takes time to sit in front of your computer to allow yourself to capture the gains of the market as it moves up and down. While some of the markets can be traded into the evening and overnight, most of them are open only during the mornings and early afternoons. This means that in order to day trade you would have to be available to follow news, read charts, and place trades during these hours. It is possible, however, to trade part-time. Some trades can be made on Sunday afternoons and after work during the week. If you would like to begin your day trading on a part-time basis, then this would be a good option for you. Just allow yourself enough time to learn the market on your shortened schedule.

Risk Tolerance

You should give some thought as to the amount of risk you are willing to take on before you begin a day trading career. Not only is there risk involved with the ups and downs of the market (and the possibility of the ups and downs of your fortunes), but there is the risk that comes from opportunity risk. This opportunity risk comes in the form of the possibility that you might be a day trader who makes a living day trading full-time, passing up the opportunity to earn a steady, relatively risk-free paycheck from working at your regular job.

Investment banks and proprietary day trading firms use a complicated mathematical formula to monitor the amount, or risk, they have involved in their trading accounts. This formula is called value at risk and frequently is recalculated so often that a bank's trading risk can be adjusted daily.

Day trading by nature involves a certain amount of risk. You are risking money to make a living. It is as simple as that. Some careers offer very little risk of your money while in the process of earning a paycheck. This is not the case with day trading. You might have the opportunity risk of not earning your living working at your safe, steady job. You will need to learn that you will be putting up your capital—your money—in order to make more money. You will be taking on risk in an effort to gain a reward in the form of profits. It is said that risk leads to reward. This means that the more you risk, the greater the potential for reward. The key word here is *potential* for reward. You should know your risk tolerance before you begin day trading. You should re-evaluate your risk tolerance before every trading day and before every trade. Your goal should be to risk as small an amount possible while gaining the greatest amount. Each trade should be set up with the knowledge that the trade will go bad. You should calculate ahead of time how much it is possible to lose on the trade, i.e., the worst-case scenario. You should keep in mind that you are trading money—money that might be put to better use than this particular trade. As with emotions, risk can be managed.

There is a whole science to **risk management** involving trade size, money management, and market knowledge. It is possible to make trades while day trading that are very risky. It is also possible to hedge all of your risk away, where as you are taking measures leading to very little risk during a trade, along with the possibility of gaining very little profit. You, as the day trader, must learn how to use a little math, market knowledge, and common sense to reach a happy, profitable balance between the two.

Available Funds

When work is done, some form of equipment is usually required. If you are a plumber, you might need a van to haul your plumbing equipment. If you are a painter, you might need brushes and ladders. If you are an accountant, you might need computers, adding machines, and tax software. When you are a day trader, your equipment is your trading account. Your trading account is usually filled with a combination of cash and margin. Just as a plumber needs a certain size van, you will need a certain amount of money to day trade with. To begin with, it doesn't have to be much. You can have a lot of fun and learn a lot with as little as $250 in your account.

For example, if you have $250 in your foreign exchange trading account you could spend the night making small, quick trades while watching TV. It is possible to do this each night and to make enough money to pay for your breakfast doughnut, lunch, and afternoon coffee all on the profits you make from the night before. This can actually be a really good way to get used to the market lingo, software, and the process of order entry all while building a positive trading experience. It can be a really rewarding experience to at first begin to learn how to trade with smaller amounts. It takes a lot of confidence and willpower to place trades big enough to draw a salary against.

Resist the temptation to think that just because you have a smaller dollar amount in your trading account that you should make high risk/reward ratio trades. Improper position size, margin mismanagement, and a series of misplaced trades can lead to losses that close out even the smallest accounts.

If you start small, and get used to the feeling of winning a trade you actually planned, you can gradually add to your account and trade larger and larger amounts. You will, however, need to have enough money set aside from your normal household budget to trade with. It is not wise to trade with your rent or car payment money. You should trade with money that is earmarked for your trading account, i.e., it should be money that you are able to lose, or at least use for a risky venture such as day trading. After you are up and running as a full-time professional day trader, you will be able to make bi-weekly or monthly withdrawals from your account as a salary draw. Until then, the money you trade with should be allowed to grow with each winning trade.

Can You Work Alone?

After you determine that you can temper your emotion, know your risk tolerance, and have disposable cash to trade with, the question will remain if you can work alone. Day trading is often done alone. Day traders often trade in an office in their homes, away from the business and financial districts of their hometowns or nearby cities. You might find that you miss the interaction of fellow co-workers, the friendly chats with other commuters on the train going to work, or even the act of walking down to the corner coffee shop with an office friend for a much-needed afternoon break. You will basically be working alone all of the time.

Not only does this mean that you will not have co-workers to speak with about last night's game, you will also not be able to discuss your trading ideas with an office mate. You might even find yourself wishing that you could approach a manager or boss about a trade you are about to make with more than the usual amount of your money involved. In these cases you might find it comforting to have a superior to help shoulder the burden of your decisions. This is not the case in day trading. All the cash, knowledge, skill, and risk taking are yours and only yours.

While it might be easy to think of the benefits of day trading and working on your own (and there are many!), you should consider the nature of the business. Here are some of the issues to consider when working alone as a day trader:

- There is no one checking your attendance.
- There is no one to make sure you are on time to be at your desk for the opening bell.
- There is no accounting department to record your gains and losses.
- There is no technical department to fix your software/computer when they don't work.
- There is no one to delegate work to: printing, faxing, filing, or running out for sandwiches.
- There is no such thing as a paid sick day—either you day trade or you don't make money!
- There is absolutely no need for nice clothes to wear to the office (good or bad, depending upon your point of view).

Like most day traders, you will probably decide that the issues with working alone are not that bad. In fact, the list of benefits that come from successfully day trading goes far and beyond the bad issues that you might encounter. Most of the real issues associated with working alone relate to your ownership of your trading account and your trades, and the lack of a social aspect.

You are the only one who makes the decisions about your day trading career and your account. There are no performance reviews. The only performance review will be your own satisfaction that you are building up your account (and net worth) through your day trading efforts. It is best to think of your day trading as a business. Show up for work at regularly scheduled times. Wear your "work clothes" if this gives you a more professional attitude, as this might give yourself a signal that you are on the clock. Give yourself periodic reviews of your trading activity. Schedule vacations with family or friends at regular times throughout the year, just like a normal job. Just having a routine of walking to the neighborhood coffee shop at the market close can lead to refreshing contact with other people.

Like a regular job, think of your day trading career as promoting from within. The promotions come in the form of getting the opportunity to take on added responsibility by trading in different, more advanced sectors. Of course, there are the promotions that come from day trading with an account that grows larger with each and every winning trade!

Support Groups

As you gain day trading experience with time, you will inevitably experience the ups and downs of the market, and good and bad economic news. You will experience times when the market is screaming ahead, and it seems as though anyone and everyone is trading and making money. You'll also develop memories of the worst trading days imaginable, when it seemed there was no rhyme or reason to the market's hysteria. A good support group can help you enjoy the good and get through the bad, and overall add to a positive day trading career.

Impersonal Groups

There are many instances that impersonal groups work in such a way as to offer enjoyment, a feeling of belonging and comfort. The news outlets are such a group. The following of a big event on TV news shows such as CNBC can lead to a feeling that you are not alone; rather, you are part of the entire financial world. With the news show's interviews and live footage from the world's trading pits, you can get a feeling that what you are doing in your private trading office or area is very much connected to the fate and fortunes of others.

It can be very enjoyable to take a minute from your trading day and watch a short story on what you have been trading. For example, you might be trading gold, capturing profits as the price of the metal moves up throughout the day. You know that gold is in the world's traders' minds, as it has been on the market and economic news feeds all day long. CNBC could break with a story from the gold pit at one of the exchanges, or possibly an interview with a major gold producer or investor. Just taking the time to see others day trading or otherwise working in the financial markets can give you a feeling of belonging to the outside world and give you a "big picture" perspective.

You can also consider reading the many periodicals available, and using this as your support group. Daily newspapers such as the *Wall Street Journal* are geared toward reporting the news much like CNBC is, but the articles offer a greater depth. Some of the monthly trade publications such as *SFO Magazine* are written specifically for both full- and part-time day traders. *SFO* is especially good, as almost every issue addresses the problems that you might encounter while day trading, including money management, seasonal position trading, and the monthly article analyzing "what went wrong." This can be a great help to the beginner as well as the expert trader looking for examples from others.

Professional and Family Support Groups

A good source to find groups and other day traders is through a professional social network such as LinkedIn. After establishing an account at *www.linkedin.com*, you can begin to sign up to get daily and weekly newsletters from day trading and various sector groups. For example, you could join a foreign exchange trading group, a quant finance group, a gold group, and an oil traders group.

Once you are in the groups, you can search through the listings of other members in the group and request that they become part of your professional network. You can be as focused or as liberal with your connections as you would like (some people have well over 500-plus connections). Day trading stories and ideas can be easily exchanged, as communication between your connections is simple. These professional networks can alert you to what others in the day trading profession are doing, what they think about current economic news, and what they are currently favoring in their trades. The overall effect can be quite refreshing; you could be studying charts on a Saturday afternoon for the next week's trades as you get an alert that you have an e-mail from one of your day trading buddies.

FACT

You can find support groups wherever you look. You can find people talking about the markets at the store, the gym, or on the train. When you look for it, you can find that the markets are on the minds of all kinds of people everywhere.

These trading friends can be from all over the world. You might hear from someone in New York who is trying to get her own hedge fund started by day trading S&P futures, you could hear from a commodities trader based in Chicago, or you could hear from a research expert based out of Zurich, Switzerland. The communication among your professional groups can act as a virtual "club" where you can meet others from the comfort of your home office.

The other obvious support group that should not be overlooked is your connection to your family and friends who are not involved with trading. It can be quite nice to take time off from a crazy week of trading to go out with your non-trader friends and family. You could go to the beach, ride bicycles in the park, go to the art museum, or even go for a walk in your nearby city's shopping district. It really does help to get away from the world of electronic trading, fast-happening news, and the constant emotional upheaval of day trading. Your family and friends can act as a way of reminding you to keep it all in perspective. The overall effect of riding a bike with friends or family to the farmer's market, or buying a cup of coffee from a vendor and sitting in the park to talk can really change your perspective. You will have to learn how to get out, and enjoy life beyond Monday through Friday's pursuit of profits. At first you might not see the value of such activity, but as you become successful as a trader, you will see this as a very necessary part of the day trading lifestyle.

Other Responsibilities

Before you consider your fit with day trading and decide if day trading is for you, you will need to consider your other responsibilities. These responsibilities can be time-oriented, money-oriented, and risk-oriented.

> The more responsibilities and restraints you have on your time, money, and risk allowance, the more stressful day trading will become. Keep day trading a relatively fun endeavor by scaling back on the dollar amount at risk during difficult or stressful periods in your life.

Time Responsibilities

Time-oriented responsibilities come down to the fact that you may have family or other obligations that do not allow you to devote enough time to day trading. Perhaps you have a young family that needs to be taken care of during the day. Taking care of small children might take up most of your day, leaving you with only small amounts of time to study the market and place trades. If this is the case, perhaps you could trade part-time in the foreign exchange markets, which are open twenty-four hours a day from Sunday night until Friday afternoon. You could build market knowledge by reading about the market during your breaks during the day, or listen to market news while going about the daily duties of taking care of your family. Your knowledge of the market can really add up over time, and this is a good way to stay fresh and up with the current news stories.

Money and Risk Responsibilities

Perhaps you are in the situation that you are very interested in day trading but you have a limited amount of cash to day trade with, or you are in a situation where you are unable to assume the additional risks that day trading brings. In these instances, you can gain a lot of market knowledge by opening up and using one of the many free "demo" accounts offered through brokers. You can start out with an imaginary deposit into the account and place real time trades using the same software and order-entry system as a live account. Many brokers offer demo accounts as a way to try trading platforms (the trading software a broker uses), or for the day trader to try trading ideas without risking real money. Do not disregard the "play-money" aspect of these demo accounts, as they can be a great tool to develop market and day trading knowledge.

Backup Plan

The last thing to consider before you start to day trade is if you have a clearly defined backup plan. This is the Plan B that you can fall on if the markets get especially nasty, and you (and other day traders) find it more and more difficult to make profitable trades with your risk tolerance. For example, in the late spring through early summer of 2010, European nations were having an especially difficult time related to sovereign debt (debt issued by individual countries). Europe's common currency, the euro, had been losing value against the U.S. dollar for weeks. Over one particular weekend, UBS (a major Swiss-based investment bank and brokerage house) reported that the euro would fall further before rebounding in six to nine months. They stated the performance of the euro was "disappointing." That same weekend, the news feed service Market Watch (*www.marketwatch.com*) made the comment that the following week might be a very difficult one for stock, oil, and currency traders, appealing only to day traders who could profit with extreme volatility.

FACT

During some times of the year it can be especially difficult to day trade. For example, stocks report their earnings quarterly, during what is often called earnings season. During **earnings season**, companies can exceed or miss what the market expected their profits to be, and this can lead to exaggerated and unpredictable price movements in a stock's price.

In this instance, you would be well served if you had a backup plan to provide yourself with some form of riskless activity to keep you out of the situation of trying to day trade in that kind of market. Perhaps you have in your backup plan an additional source of income. When the market is like this, having a plan to make money away from your trading desk can really help in keeping your trading account safe and profitable.

Times like these could also offer you the opportunity to take some of the profits from your account and take a vacation, or do something else with your time and money beyond getting into the trap of fighting the market. With the market's past events, such as falling currencies, banking crises, and wild, unpredictable news stories rocking the markets, sometimes it is just better to take your profits and walk away from trading for a while. While day trading involves putting your money at some kind of risk, your money does *not* always have to be in a risky situation. You will have to know ahead of time that it is acceptable to not day trade from time to time. You will need to have a plan what to do with your time and your money when (not if!) this time comes.

CHAPTER 4

Getting Set Up for Trading

Once you have learned the basics of the markets, day trading, and how a day trader spends her day, you will need to move to the point of getting set up for trading. It is not wise to just jump right into buying and selling in an account without first writing a business plan, setting up an office, and selecting a computer. Having a basic overview of your software and information requirements will also go a long way in getting yourself set up for day trading.

Writing a Business Plan

It is important to begin your day trading career with the full intention that it is a business. Although your day trading business might start out as your part-time job, it should be set up in such a way as to be profitable and tax efficient. The best way to establish these goals is through the writing and use of a business plan.

Business Plan Basics

A business plan is a formal document that you can use to establish the direction and purpose of your day trading business. Although the plan can be changed as you develop, the business plan should serve as your road map as to how to get from A to B. Your A might be just starting out: learning about the markets and day trading, opening an account, funding your account, and your first three to six months of successful trading. Your B can be turning your part-time day trading job into your full-time career.

Think of writing your business plan as a tool that you will be using to ask a bank to invest in your company. With this in mind, you should treat the writing of the business plan as an essential tool to have before your first trade is made. This will force you to do the required research and training to ensure a high level of success at your day trading.

After you get your business plan written, you should then consider yourself in business. Most businesses exist with the thought of being a profitable venture. In the course of making profits, a business usually encounters expenses. When thinking of your company, think of all of the parts that go into making it possible to trade. The expense of books, newspapers, cable, furniture, as well as the cost of meals out can be an expense if they are related to the operation of your day trading business. Your business plan should establish in your mind that you are running a company, and not everything will be profits and income; there will be expenses, too. These expenses should be part of the business plan, and if planned properly, can be not that bad, as they can reduce your overall tax burden at the end of the year.

You business plan should include the following:

▼ TOPICS IN YOUR BUSINESS PLAN

Topic of Business Plan	Content
Company Mission	Your goals of getting from A to B
A Description of the Company's Service	Day trading what markets
Management Team Description	Your background, computer skills, and market knowledge
Equipment	List of equipment needs of the company
Furthering Education	Description of procedures to gain further market knowledge
Profit Goals	Procedures as to when to take profits
Risk Management	Procedures to limit risk: margin, position size, and pyramid method
Capital Requirements	Initial funding requirements, scheduled capital contributions
Capital Withdrawals	Procedures for scheduling withdrawals from your trading account

Setting Up an Office

You can set up your office wherever it is convenient for you. Your office might be an entirely separate room in your home. This room could be a converted extra bedroom or even a converted formal dining room. It need not be formally furnished, but the furnishings must be adequate to hold your books, TV stand, computer, and other equipment. You can even use part of a room if you live in a small space and you would like to double up on the usage of your living area. The only real requirement is that you are comfortable and have good lighting. It's even possible to have a completely portable office where you are able to temporarily move your computer from your reading and research area of your home to the couch. With your portable office, you can casually trade at night while sitting on the couch.

If you have the right equipment, you can have a safe, secure Internet connection, even at your local coffee shop or other public location. It can be a lot of fun to start the day early and begin trading in the early hours of the morning, walk to Starbucks or Caribou Coffee, fire up your computer, and begin trading as the morning sun comes in through the windows.

There are stories of day traders walking to the corner, unloading their computers and trading logs, and beginning to trade at 5:30 A.M. At this early hour they can capture the busiest hours of the foreign exchange (FX or Forex) market, or read all of the overnight news for the commodities and stock market. The old adage "the early bird gets the worm" can really ring true in this instance. You can greet the local early morning regulars as they get their coffee on their way to their jobs while you study the market's developments. With today's modern technology, your office can be anywhere you get a secure Internet connection.

Market knowledge is gained with time and practice. Perhaps you do not want to trade with your big account without the controlled environment of your home office. In this instance you could use your practice or demo account to stay on top of the markets but also spend some time away from your usual work place.

Equipment

Just as a plumber needs his van and a painter needs his brushes, you will need the proper equipment to day trade. This equipment consists of furniture, a phone, and cable access TV.

The first grouping of equipment is the furniture. It is not necessary to invest a lot of money in furniture and lighting. The goal should be to provide yourself with an environment where you can concentrate on the work at hand: day trading. With this in mind, you will need adequate lighting, chairs, and desks.

If you are setting up an office for the first time, you can shop around to find affordable, quality work-minded furnishings at a store such as IKEA, Affordable Portables, and office supply stores such as OfficeMax or Office Depot. IKEA and other office furnishing stores can offer a variety of modern and efficient desks and computer stations as well as comfortable, ergonomic chairs and lighting. In addition to office furniture, you should include access to telephone, TV, and the Internet. Your cell phone can act as your office phone, as this will cut down on your monthly expenses—you can generally report the usage of your office phone as a tax write off.

Access to cable TV can be of great use. You can start your day by listening to the business news stations, such as CNBC or Bloomberg, while you get ready for the morning. They can offer some very good insight as to what economic reports are scheduled to happen later on in the day. This can serve as a good way to get into day trading early, before some of the markets open. The combination of a strong cup of coffee or tea and a review of the markets with this method can help you recognize some very profitable day trading opportunities that are coming along in the latter part of the day. It could also alert you as to the fact that the markets are in a state of unrest.

This unrest can be due to what happened overnight in the Asian or European markets, or the fact that a big U.S. economic report is coming out. In this case, a typical scenario could follow: You wake up at 4:30 A.M., start the coffeemaker, read the "Markets" Section of the *Wall Street Journal*, and casually watch the morning news shows. You could be informed that overnight the markets in Germany and London were in disarray, and at 2 P.M. this afternoon the U.S. Federal Reserve will make an announcement on U.S. interest rates. Armed with this information, you could decide that it is in your best interest to take the day off from active day trading with the following effects: 1) You would miss out on any upside from potential positive news made during the day, and 2) You would insulate yourself from any whipsawing, or wild swings back and forth in the markets preceding and following major news. You could decide that no profit (but keeping your trading account intact) is better than risking your account on a big news day.

Computer Hardware and Software

One of the key ingredients to your day trading business will be your computer hardware and software. Although the computer hardware offered by most retailers is constantly being upgraded and improved, there are some basic requirements to be met.

Laptop computers have developed to the point where an off-the-shelf version can have a powerful enough microprocessor and enough memory to handle day trading.

▼ HARDWARE SPECIFICATIONS AND BENEFITS

Hardware Requirement	Benefits to Your Trading
1GHz or higher microprocessor	Speed. The horsepower of your computer—the higher the microprocessor speed, the better it will handle all of the trading screens, research reports, news articles, and charts that are open at the same time.
2–4 gigs of RAM	The more RAM your computer has, the faster it will allow you to process your buy and sell orders, and upload information and reports from the Internet.
15-inch screen	The bigger the screen, the more room you have to open up additional applications, such as trading input areas, charts, and news screens at the same time.
High-speed Internet	The backbone that connects your computer to your broker's order input area—it is essential that it is as fast as possible and private (no shared networks or public-access Internet connections).

In order to day trade effectively, you will not go wrong in the purchase and use of one of the many quality laptops available in technology stores. Internet connections can be DSL, cable, or wireless and directly connected to your computer (G3 or G4, depending upon your service area).

Trading software, or the **trading platform**, is usually provided to you by your broker. In fact, the choice of brokers often has direct ties to the quality, efficiency, and ease of their software, including the presentation and creation of technical charts and the order-entry system.

After research, you might choose three or four brokerages for a test run of their software offerings. It is easy to open up a demo account, download the software (trading platform), and try it out for a few weeks. You will be using play money, of course, but you will get the hang of the tools provided by the brokerage. After you have decided upon which brokerage you would like to keep, you can allow the other demo accounts to expire, and remove them from your computer.

Requirements for Trading Platforms

Trading platforms should provide all the tools you need to trade, but at the same time be as simple as possible, and not have an overly technical or cluttered appearance.

You should find the order-entry system and method to be simple to use and somewhat intuitive, preferably with provisions to enter in trades other than market orders. While market orders are trades that are filled with whatever price the market is at that time, other types of orders might have a predetermined, set buy and/or sell price, where the order will only be filled at these specific limits. As you get more familiar with day trading and get into more advanced trading techniques, you will discover that this feature is an absolute must have, and should not be overlooked.

The technical charts provided should allow an adjustment for different timeframes with the click of a button. For example, you could be analyzing a potential trade in the S&P 500 futures and be looking at a thirty-second chart, or a chart that shows different changes up or down with thirty-second intervals. To gain a broader perspective, it is good practice to change the timeframe of the same chart to longer intervals, such as five minutes, fifteen minutes, one hour, and one day. With the ability to change the timeframes of your charts in this manner, you are better able to see the bigger picture, and therefore see more potential day trading trends and ideas.

The second characteristic you should be looking for in your broker's trading platform is the quality of the technical chart properties. The properties should include the availability to switch from bar chart to candlestick, and the option for indicator overlays. The switch from bar chart to candlestick chart will change the type of information you will be able to gather from reading the charts, such as previous opening and closing prices or volumes. The availability of indicators would allow you to draw lines over the longer timeframe charts to view trends visually. For example, you could use your chart software to draw a line on a chart and see a pattern such as a breach of a key support level, i.e., a point at which a security has fallen below a statistical (and often psychological) lowest point before a rapid sell off to lower levels.

Periodical and Newspaper Subscriptions

In addition to your equipment, and computer hardware and software, you will find that reading the various business and trading periodicals will act as an integral part of getting set up for your day.

Reading about Trading

You will be day trading in markets that are changing week to week, day to day, and hour to hour. In order to day trade effectively in this constantly shifting arena, you will need to have both a strategic view of how the market works, and a tactical, short-term view of where the market is going. You can gain a very broad knowledge of how businesses, economies, and markets function together by keeping a strict reading and studying schedule. You could schedule reading of books, newspapers, and magazines related to day trading for certain parts of your work week. With a set schedule, you can get a lot accomplished with your goal of becoming savvy about where the economy is, where it is going, and how it relates to the markets you trade in. Remember, you are searching for clues as to what offers a good trading opportunity. You should also have a defensive goal of knowing what is going on in the world economy and world markets to allow you to sidestep any pitfalls in trading, i.e., the avoidance of any bad trades.

Get into the Habit of Studying

Once you get into the habit of studying, you will look for the opportunity to study whenever you can in regard to your day trading business. You might subscribe to and read the *Wall Street Journal* in the morning before you begin to trade, and switch to a monthly magazine such as *SFO* during your off days when you're not trading, and polish your technical chart reading skills by reading *The Active Trader* while spending time with your family in the park. You could even find yourself spending your time listening to audio versions of the various periodicals and the on-air news magazines, such as NPR's *Market Place* or WBBM's (AM 780) *Noon Business Hour* (Midwest Market). There are also downloadable online versions of *Money Talk*, a nationally syndicated on-air magazine devoted exclusively to the markets and money matters. You would be surprised how much knowledge you can pick up in relation to the markets and economic matters that can be directly tied to your day trading career.

Smarter Than the Other Guy

You must remember that for each trade you make, there is someone making the opposite trade. With each buy you make, someone is selling, and with each sell you make, someone is buying. It is important for you to never underestimate the "other guy's" market knowledge. When you learn to day trade, what you are actually doing is learning how to notice situations in which you can make money by going along with others' ideas or against others' ideas. The markets are, by nature, very difficult to navigate; any skill you acquire along the way can help improve your results and add to your profitability and enjoyment of day trading. By day trading, you are competing against some of the brightest minds on Wall Street (actually, worldwide), and the most powerful computers. You are competing against Northwestern University and Wharton School of Business MBAs, and complex algorithmic computer programs written by PhDs. On the flip side of these advanced degrees and micro-processor speeds is the fact that *even the brightest minds can call the market wrong!* Keep this in mind when you are gaining skills in your day trading arsenal. Take your time to build up your market knowledge over the weeks, months, and years. And remember, you are always someone else's "other guy."

Trading News Feed Services

In addition to your daily and monthly periodical reading list, you should include the following daily reviews of some of the day trading news feed services and brokers' reports.

Independent News Feeds

Depending upon the broker you choose, you will generally have access to a markets'- and economics-related news source. These are usually more in-depth and focused than the market news that can be accessed from the same companies' free websites. For example, your broker might offer a news wire that is broken down into the following sections:

- Equities
- Currencies
- Commodities
- Gold and Silver
- Economics
- Exchange Traded Funds
- Futures
- Politics and Policies
- Europe
- Asia
- Banking and Credit

The news service would have staff reporters all over the world available to report on the sector news as it developed over the course of the trading day (and night). If you were day trading gold, for example, you could click on the Gold and Silver section and find anywhere from one to ten articles on the development of the gold market, its current London close, mining output, Central bank purchases and sales, gold ETFs tonnages, and any other recent information that is related to gold. Articles are usually stored for a week or so, so you can quickly get a sense of where the market was and therefore make a conclusion of where it is going. Due to the almost informal nature of the articles, even the smallest amount of news is reported several times during the day. A story on gold reaching a new high can be followed on an almost per-hour basis, along with supporting articles on the mood of traders from London, New York, and Dubai, as well as volume reports, etc.

Broker Published Research

In addition to the independent news feeds, your broker will most likely offer daily, weekly, monthly, and quarterly research reports of various lengths and depths. They might offer an early morning market commentary that would serve to inform you of their best day trading ideas across all markets. Your broker could also offer a supplemental special report on the direction of main-day trade sectors such as foreign exchange, commodities, and equities. Monthly and quarterly reports could focus on long-term market conditions, economics, or day trading education memos.

These broker reports almost take the form of advisory memos and can really help you in deciding entry (buy) and exit (sell) points for a trade. They can also help you get a feel for how the market is moving over time, as you can look back over the weeks and see a story develop as the reports are written. For example, you could read a three or four week report of the weakness of the U.S. dollar as compared to the euro, and follow the story of how the dollar gained ground over the European currency, gradually to the point where day traders all over the world were worried of future weakening of the euro with thoughts of "when will this end" and "if I only shorted the euro!"

Studying the Market's News over Time

This brings up another point: When you first get into day trading, everything will be new. You will get the impression that the market will always be the way it is today, the S&P will always be this high, gold will never come back, the dollar is dead, etc. When you study the markets over time and develop trading experience, you will see that everything is constantly moving. Sometimes it seems as though the market has its own will, and that will is one of an unruly child, subject to fits of anger, upheaval, and only occasional discipline. This is actually a good thing, as movement in the markets creates day trading opportunities. You will recognize what market is good to trade in at what times, when it's better to **go long**, and when it's better to **go short**.

For example, the Switzerland-based brokerage house and financial advisor UBS issued a report in the late fall of 2007 that the world's currencies were out of whack, and that some of the most popular day trading currencies such as the New Zealand dollar (NZD) and Australian dollar (AUD) had become way overvalued against the U.S. dollar (USD) and the Japanese yen (JPY). UBS predicted an unwinding of the massive long AUD/JPY, AUD/USD, NZD/JPY, and NZD/USD positions in traders' accounts worldwide. Since those trades had developed their disproportionate and extreme values over many years, the prediction was that the correction would come suddenly and inevitably. The trigger point for such a massive unwinding was the housing crisis and the banking crisis that followed. All of a sudden, traders were selling risky, high-yielding currencies such as the AUD and NZD, and buying USD and JPY. Problems were compounded when the central banks of Australia and New Zealand lowered their interest rates dramatically and suddenly, which further lessened the appeal of the commodity currencies. Almost two years later, the two currency pairs were back in alignment, with UBS issuing reports to again go long on AUD and NZD. With your market knowledge and trading experience developed over time, you could see the beginning of a new, long-term trend and trading opportunity.

CHAPTER 5

Sectors to Day Trade

Picking sectors to day trade is like picking out clothes. Most people choose clothes depending on their environments—easy-going jeans on a lazy day, a sport coat on a trip to Europe, or a parka in the freezing cold. Market sectors are always rotating, and there is always something in play. You need to know what's available to trade, whether it's ETFs, foreign exchange, or commodities. You need to know what is hot in what season, what fits your plan, and the benefits and pitfalls of each sector.

Stocks

Before you begin to day trade, you will first need to determine what you would like to trade. There are several sectors of good day tradable products to choose from. The first sector to consider day trading is stocks. Stocks are a good place to start because it is easy to understand what exactly is going to be traded.

Pieces of a Company

Stocks are representations of the net worth of a public company. Each public company divides its value by a certain number of pieces, or shares. Each share represents part ownership in that particular company. A share of XYZ Company is the legal equivalent of part ownership of every desk, truck, building, and piece of property on XYZ's balance sheet.

Stocks are divided into groups depending upon their **market cap**. The market cap is the number of shares outstanding in the market times the price of the share. For example, if XYZ Company has 1 million shares outstanding, and each share of XYZ stock is $10, the market cap of XYZ is $10 million or 1,000,000 x $10.

A share of stock also represents part ownership of any future profits XYZ Company will make while doing business. The value of share of stock is calculated by a complex formula, but basically, a share of XYZ Company's stock amounts to this: the public's estimate of the value of XYZ's future cash flows. In other words, if a stock analyst at Goldman Sachs thinks that A Company will produce more cash through the normal course of business than B Company (and both A and B are in the same industry), then A Company will be worth more than B Company, and A's shares of stock will also be worth more than B's stock.

The Problem with Stock Analysis

The problem with the stock analysis formula is the most important variable in the complex formula is actually an *educated guess!* This "guess" about cash flows leads to different calculated valuations of the stock, leading to different traders valuing the stock as "expensive" (overvalued) or "cheap" (undervalued).

If a trader thinks of a stock as cheap, she will buy it, and if a different trader thinks of the stock as expensive, he will sell it. A stock's price will move up and down as it is bought and sold, as if it is caught in a constant tug-of-war. This action creates an opportunity for you as the day trader to ride the movements up and down, piggyback-style, capturing profits as you move in and out of the trades.

Stock Market Cap and Day Trading

Mega caps and large caps are well-known, widely traded stocks that offer relative safety in their trading. They usually have a limited upside, but this limited upside can be a small price to pay for the benefit of being a safe bet, as mega and large caps usually move *with* the market. In other words, when people are saying "the market was up today," or when CNBC reports the S&P 500 has had a strong day, you can most likely rest assured that the mega and large caps have also had an up day.

There is a certain good feeling you get when you know that pension funds, mutual funds, and hedge funds all over the world are interested in trading your popular, large cap stock. Their interest in trading your security adds volume and price support, and effectively breathes life into your chosen security. Small cap stocks are less traded, have less volume, and are prone to larger, less frequent price movements. Small cap stocks move so little that they are frequently used as a training tool for hedge funds and other investment companies. These institutions often have young, fresh, Ivy League MBAs sit and watch small cap stocks on trading screens where nothing will happen for days, giving the newer employees time to get used to looking for setups, entry points, and exit points. Also, it takes training to get mentally strong enough to concentrate on a fast moving computer screen for hours while large sums of money are at risk. The banks like to get the new recruits used to paying attention for long hours in front of a slow moving screen before they move into trading with and risking larger amounts of the trading capital.

The Pros and the Cons of Day Trading Stocks

One of the benefits of day trading stocks is that they are easy to research. Almost all brokerages offering day trading capabilities allow access to high-quality, in-house research that can be cross checked with the research put out by independent firms. Second, trading individual stocks offers the opportunity for large percentage movements when a stock is **in play**.

A stock (or other investment) is in play when some news has come out on the company, and the news has caused other traders to take notice. When other traders take notice, a stock will go up or down, depending on whether the news is perceived to be good or bad for the company. These can lead to exciting times, as the day trader can be trading the stock while hearing about it on news stations such as CNBC, and then reading about the stock's activity in papers such as the *Wall Street Journal* the next day. This feeling of being a part of the news as it happens is one of the fun parts of the day trading lifestyle.

A downside of day trading individual stocks is the tendency of traders to develop a trading portfolio of undiversified positions, which leads to concentration risk. Think of the "don't put too many of your eggs in one basket" adage. While this might lead to large losses (or gains!), it doesn't always. Sometimes a stock in your trading portfolio can be "stuck in the mud" and fall out of other traders' sights, leading to stagnant trading days. Your money could be tied up in a stock that doesn't move enough to make a profitable trade, while putting that amount of your tradable cash or margin at risk of being a bad trade while you wait. A second drawback of day trading stocks is that your margin is greatly limited as compared to FX or futures. Think of *margin* as a form of revolving credit card to day trade with. There are regulations as to the amount of margin (or credit) you can use for different sectors. Some sectors, like stocks, are limited to a small amount, around 50 percent of your stock position. Some sectors allow very large margin amounts, such as foreign exchange, which can have limits up to 50,000 percent of your position.

Exchange Traded Funds

Exchange traded funds, or ETFs, are instruments that are "baskets" of individual stocks or other underlying products. They are subject to the same valuation procedures as individual stocks, but offer the diversification function of a mutual fund.

Diversification and Concentration Benefits

The mutual fund–like property of ETFs can be a real advantage, as the diversified basket reduces the concentration risk of individual stocks. At the same time, when you day trade ETFs you can capture the price movements of an entire industry sector such as financial company stocks, oil company stocks, or technology/biotechnology stocks. Certain sectors are in play at different times, and are influenced by different factors. With this in mind, day trading ETFs can offer a very neat, compact, and effective way to trade a whole sector when that sector is moving rapidly and in play.

You can use an ETF to day trade almost any type of position you can imagine. There are even ETFs that offer a "short" position, allowing you to make money when the ETFs basket of stocks goes down in value. These ETFs are often called *bears*, after the *bulls* and *bears* name of the stock market's buyers and sellers.

The Pros and Cons of Day Trading ETFs

Some of the good things about day trading ETFs include diversification, multiple sector availability, and popularity with traders and institutional investors. Popularity with traders and institutional investors can lead to relative safety and overall good day trading opportunities. The few disadvantages to day trading ETFs are mainly limited to the fact that your trading margin will be restricted to the same amount as individual stocks, as ETFs are traded on the same exchanges as most individual stocks, and are regulated as such.

Foreign Exchange

After you leave the relatively simple world of individual stocks and ETFs, you might want to enter the world of day trading foreign exchange, gold, commodities, and futures. These sectors can allow a day trader to amplify each trade, as the allowable margin ratios can be quite large, and in some cases unbelievably so.

What Sets Foreign Exchange Apart

Day trading in the foreign exchange (FX) market lately has become one of the preferred areas for traders looking to make a living at trading. It is an unregulated market, open around the world, trading twenty-four hours a day from Sunday afternoon to Friday afternoon. Trading FX differs from other types of trading in a variety of ways. The first difference is what is being traded: As opposed to companies, baskets of companies, or a commodity, what you are trading is the difference between the exchange rates of two currencies. For example, you could place trades thinking the Australian dollar will strengthen against the Japanese yen (AUD/JPY), the U.S. dollar strengthening against the Swiss franc (USD/CHF), or the Norwegian krone getting stronger against the euro (NOK/EUR). You sell, or short, the currency you think will go down, and use the money to buy, or long, the currency you think will go up.

Advantages to Day Trading FX

One benefit of day trading FX is the low minimum account openings. Some brokerages allow you to open with $25 and some as low as $1. How can trades with such low amounts be made effectively? It's because FX margin ratios can be anywhere from 10:1 to as much as 500:1. That means you could trade $50,000 worth of currency with only $100 in your account. As you can see, FX traders have a bit of a "Wild West" mentality: there is a lot of money to be made even with small account balances.

Also, due to the limited amount of currency pairs available (EUR/USD, AUD/JPY, CAD/USD, etc.), there is a lot less to study and learn, and you can quickly get a feel for the market. It's relatively easy to analyze trends in the FX market when you're looking for trading ideas. FX lends itself well to both economic and news analysis as well as technical chart trends. Traders look to the economic reports published by the major world central banks to value the currency pairs. Also, the study of technical charts can easily show when a currency pair is stretched and due for a correction.

Some currency "pairs" such as AUD/JPY are classically known as measures of stock trader's risk appetite and move in tandem with the world's stock markets. When the world's traders feel they want to accept more risk into their portfolios and buy more stock, the high-yielding, risky Australian dollar will also appreciate against the lower-yielding, safer Japanese yen.

Central banks are very aware of when their country's currency gets over- or undervalued in relation to its main trading partners. Banks can, and often do, intervene in the currency markets to force the adjustment of their currency. This is called **quantitative easing**, and it can cause rapid movements in the nation's currency. Quantitative easing can create a wonderful day trading opportunity, because a whole country's financial reserves are working to move the markets.

The Difficulties of FX Day Trading

FX day trading does have its downside, though. The fact that things can happen quickly and unpredictably is a negative aspect of FX trading that is shared with other sectors. FX markets are subject to unpredictable impacts, such as economic and geo-political news like unemployment figures, military skirmishes, and other quickly happening, short-timeframe events. Other news and events influencing the FX market are sudden (or not so sudden) central bank interest rate changes. For example, a Pacific Rim currency such as the Australian dollar (AUD) can increase its interest rates overnight while you sleep, causing a long-lasting "jump" in the value of the currency against a lower-yielding currency such as the Swiss franc (CHF). This could cause serious problems with any short AUD/CHF positions you might have been holding overnight with thoughts that the safe-haven Swiss franc would appreciate against the high-yielding Australian dollar.

One More Thing about Day Trading FX

A factor that works both for and against you when day trading FX is the availability of such large margin amounts. Once you get used to the amount of leverage in your **FX account** and learn how to use it safely, it can be a very effective tool to amplify your profits. If used excessively, however, it can lead to large losses very quickly.

Gold as a Currency

If you are thinking that the FX market might be a good place to trade, you might also consider the gold market. Day trading gold is unique in trading, because you have to think of it as both a commodity and a currency.

Paper Money and the Price of Gold

You might be thinking that it is easy to see that gold is a commodity, as it has the physical property of being a metal. But why is gold a currency? This is because the price of gold moves inversely with the value of paper money such as the U.S. dollar, the British pound, and the euro. This is true because while there is a relatively fixed amount of gold, there is an ever-changing amount of printed and electronic money available. When there is more money in circulation, the price of gold goes up because there is more money bidding on the same amount of gold.

Study the potential for gold trading beginning in the early fall to get a feel for where the gold market will be heading—usually up! This is because physical gold is heavily purchased and given as gifts during the Indian marriage season in the fall and the Chinese New Year in the spring.

Day trading gold can be like day trading the market's sentiment on inflation. The more the market thinks there is potential for inflation, the more traders will bid up the price of gold. The opposite is also true: The more rosy and positive the economic picture, the more traders will sell gold, causing the price to go down.

The Benefits of Day Trading Gold

Trading gold can be a bit simpler to decipher than other trading markets. It's easier to read the fundamentals of a potential trade when there are relatively few influencing factors. Also, a 400-ounce brick of gold (the size of the gold bars that are stored in the vaults at Fort Knox) will *never* go bankrupt. More than a few companies have lost a majority of their value through bankruptcy in the history of the stock market. This will never happen with gold. Gold has no balance sheet, no debt, and no product to sell. Also, there is a limited amount of gold, and it will most likely be in demand for some time.

When the world's central banks buy or sell their strategic gold reserves, the sale and purchase is recorded in **book entry format.** This means that the gold bars do not actually move from vault to vault. Instead, an accounting entry is made to record the transfer. This is done because the soft 24-karat bars would wear out from all the handling!

The Problems with Day Trading Gold

However, gold prices are subject to geopolitical as well as economic news, both of which can be fast coming and unannounced (with often illogical effects on the market). Another issue that affects gold's price is that gold is strategically bought and sold by the world's central banks. An announcement from a major central bank to buy or sell large quantities of gold could move the markets quickly and for the long term, with both good and bad effects depending how you are positioned. Because of the limited amount of gold available to trade, both central banks and major institutional investors (such as hedge funds) can have a big influence on the price of gold in the market.

Lastly, the nature of gold's day tradable products, mainly ETFs and futures, offer downsides themselves: low available margin for ETFs and high minimum account size for futures.

Commodities

Commodities are also known as **raw materials** or **hard assets**. Commodities have been a day trader's dream in the past few years. Yes, they lost some of their steam after the banking crisis took hold in late 2008, but they remain traders' favorites for a variety of reasons.

Easy to Understand Movements

Commodities are well-liked because they have easy-to-understand reasons for price movement. Commodities' prices are basically related to the world's economies. When the economies of the world are doing well, the price of commodities usually go up. This upward trend can play out over days, seasons, and years. When commodities are in play, they are in play in a really big way. Below is a table of commodities, including the size of the smallest contract available, the exchange they are listed on, and the hours they are traded.

▼ **TYPES OF TRADABLE COMMODITIES**

Commodity	Contract Size	Exchange	Trading Hours
Level II Softs			
Corn	5,000 Bushels	CBOT	9:30 A.M.–1:15 P.M. Central
Oats	5,000 Bushels	CBOT	9:30 A.M.–1:15 P.M. Central
Soybeans	5,000 bushels	CBOT	9:30 A.M.–1:15 P.M. Central
Level II Metals			
Copper	25,000 lbs	CMX	8:10 A.M.–1 P.M. Eastern
Platinum	50 troy ounces	NYMEX	8:20 A.M.–1:05 P.M. Eastern
Silver	5,000 troy ounces	CMX	8:25 A.M.–1:25 P.M. Eastern
Level II Petroleums			
Light Sweet Crude Oil	1,000 barrels	NYMEX	10 A.M.–2:30 P.M. Eastern
Heating Oil No. 2	42,000 gal	NYMEX	10 A.M.–2:30 P.M. Eastern
Gasoline—NY Unleaded	42,000 gal	NYMEX	10:05 A.M.–2:30 P.M. Eastern
Natural Gas	10,000 million BTUs	NYMEX	10 a.M.–2:30 P.M. Eastern

Commodities Are Tied to the World's Economies

Commodities can be an inflation trade, like gold, but they are more directly tied to the world economy's productions. Rapidly expanding countries such as China and India have a huge demand for raw materials when their economies are moving ahead strongly. With this in mind, commodities can have a unidirectional trend in good times. This means that while the price of oil and copper go up and down on a daily basis, the net trend over an economic period will generally be up for several years. This takes a little bit of the guess out of trading . . . just think **net long** (over time, an average of more long positions than short positions), and you will capture the slowly creeping trend to more and more expensive hard assets.

Hard assets can be relatively uncorrelated to the stock market. This means that oil, corn, and copper have the potential to move independently of the stock market's everyday ups and downs. In this respect, knowing how to trade commodities can allow you to have a market to trade when traditional stock markets are trending sidewise, going nowhere, or otherwise stuck in the mud.

Factors That Affect Commodities Day Trading

Commodities can have a great seasonal aspect. Gasoline gets expensive during the summer driving months, and natural gas and heating oil get expensive in the winter months. Day trading commodities such as grains and petroleums offers opportunities to capture profits related to unpredictable extreme weather, natural and manmade disasters, and geo-political concerns. For example, the price of live cattle, hogs, and grains can be affected by heavy rains or drought in the Midwest United States; orange juice usually goes up in price after an unusual cold snap in Florida.

Petroleums can be affected by weather too: Natural gas can go up or down with colder and warmer-than-usual winters. A bitter cold winter weekend in the northeastern United States can make the price of heating oil jump as suddenly as a hurricane in the Gulf of Mexico can make the price of gasoline climb overnight. Manmade disasters like oil spills and geopolitical events such as problems in the gulf of Arabia can also affect the price of petroleum suddenly and without warning.

Rapid, sudden movements in prices are a day trader's opportunity to make profits. When a commodity, ETF, or other tradable vehicle is in play, it is always possible to make money quickly. One trading day in May 2010, the stock market made a 9-percent plunge in a matter of hours. It recovered most of its losses by the end of the day, and the next Monday the S&P went up another 4 percent! If you entered the market in the bottom and got out of the market by the end of the day, it would have been very profitable indeed. While some day traders were sweating it out, covering their positions to the downside, others were kicking themselves that they were away from the trading desk, shopping, traveling, or otherwise taking it easy that day.

One More Thing about Commodities

Another thing you should think about when considering day trading commodities: although there are a few commodities ETFs to trade, most day trading in commodities is done in the futures markets. Trading commodities futures requires large account minimums, large amounts of leverage, and early-to-mid-day trading hours. If you are starting with a small amount of money to trade at first, or are building up your skills while keeping your full-time job, perhaps you should consider commodities *after* you have made the transition to day trading as your full-time career.

Futures

When people say they trade futures they are basically saying they are trading fixed-sized contracts that allow the holder to buy or sell an underlying product at a set price at a specific date in the future.

Futures have their number of units per contract and settlement date set by the exchanges and can't be modified. This means that contracts are uniformly interchangeable, so trading is simplified. Each futures contract has a buyer and a seller. One of the parties involved in the trade will be a hedger and one will be a speculator. The hedger will enter into the contract to offset her risk that the future price of the product will move up or down against her.

For example, a manager of an airline gets the feeling that the price of jet fuel will go up substantially in the next six months, and this price increase will make it difficult for her company to make a profit. She buys an oil future with a set price of oil six months in the future in an effort to lock in the price of jet fuel for her fleet of airplanes. The set price she locks in is one that she knows that her company can afford to pay for fuel and still make an acceptable profit. With the contract, she is hedging her fuel expense risk, as it is a form of managing the future expenses and profit of the company.

The other end of her oil future contract will be bought by a speculator. This speculator does not have an actual need for oil or jet fuel. He does, however, think that the price of oil will be less in the next six months than the contract price. Seeing an opportunity to make a profit, he will buy the futures contract that the airline company manager is selling. Money is made on a futures contract when the locked in price of the contract is less than the actual price of the commodity. For example, if you buy one crude oil contract in July for oil to be delivered in November at $70 a barrel, and the actual price of crude oil moves above the $70 contract price, the value of your futures contract will move in tandem to these price movements. If oil has moved to $90 by the time the contract expires, you basically have the right to own 1,000 barrels of oil at $70 per barrel and then turn around and sell the 1,000 barrels on the market for $90 per barrel, making a profit of $20,000 or $20 x 1,000 barrels. The dollar equivalent of this transaction will be the gain in the price of your future. These contracts are bought and sold in huge quantities daily, creating a very liquid and profitable market for day trading.

Many Active Traders

Futures products range from commodities to financial products such as T-bill futures, foreign exchange futures, and S&P 500 futures. With their set contract size and delivery dates, they can be traded year round and worldwide with just an Internet connection. The futures market is deep, with many institutional traders and companies coming together, and can be truly international. A Swiss food company might enter into a U.S. dollar futures trade and offset it with the purchase of a wheat future. With this they can lock in the exchange rate from Swiss francs to U.S. dollars and plan to use the U.S. dollars to purchase #2 soft red winter wheat to ship to their foodstuffs factory in Costa Rica.

Every little bit helps! While most day traders use a system of both computer assisted and manual trading, some $100 million-plus hedge funds have mathematically based fully automatic "black box" trading platforms that are programmed to be in and out of a futures trade for under $10 in profit!

Zero-Based Futures Day Trading

As a day trader you can trade futures using large amounts of margin, which can amplify your trading profits with each trade. Futures accounts are **zero-based** with profitable and losing trades being settled at the end of each trading day. This means losses will be subtracted from your account and placed in the winner's account, and the traders holding the losing end of your winning trades will add to your account. This will effectively decrease or increase your buying power the next day, so winning trades can be compounded by buying more contracts if there is a momentum to the market. This zero-based account settling coupled with high margin can lead to highly profitable trading days. In fact, futures day trading is sometimes the method that highly leveraged, fast-moving, technology-driven hedge funds use to capture the very high returns for which they can be known.

Downsides of day trading futures include large account minimums and large contract sizes. Some of the financial futures contracts can be as large as $1 million per contract, which can be a barrier for even seasoned day traders. Additionally, the futures markets are usually opened in the mornings and closed by early afternoon. This would limit your ability to trade futures if you are building up skills while holding a full-time job.

CHAPTER 6

Deciding What to Trade

There are many sectors in which to trade, and certain sectors are more tradable during certain times of the year. It is also true that certain sectors offer great day trading opportunities for years at a stretch, to only then fall out of favor when that market slows down. With this in mind, you should trade what you like and become an expert on it. You should also know what's good to trade in what season and what's good to trade when you hold a full-time job.

Trade What You Like

When deciding what to day trade it is important to begin with a sector or investment vehicle that you like and naturally understand. This will go a long way in your studies and while trading in those markets. It is important to find something to trade that makes sense to you and that you can relate to. In this way, you will have a natural draw to that market, and that will help you in your attempts to get a feel for day trading that sector.

▼ **KNOWLEDGE OF INDUSTRIES AND DAY TRADING SECTORS**

Industry Knowledge	Sector to Day Trade
Banking, Inflation, Economics, Foreign Travel	Gold ETFs, Gold Futures, Silver ETFs, Silver Futures, FX, Currency ETFs, Currency Futures, Copper Futures, Nonfarm Payroll Futures
Fuel Costs, Energy Costs	Energy Stock ETFs, Crude Futures, Heating Oil Futures, Electricity Futures, Natural Gas Futures
Watching Your 401k's Balance, Stock Market News	S&P 500 Futures and ETFs, E-Mini Dow, Power Shares QQQ Futures and ETF, Financial Stock ETFs

The key to deciding what to trade is to determine what you are interested in, and then find a financial product that is related to its manufacture, pursuit, or process. In this manner you will have a leg up on the basics involved with that financial product or sector. You will then find it natural to look at what you are trading and how it relates to the outside world beyond your electronic trading screen. When you are trading what you like and are naturally drawn to, you will find it easier to think about the subject of day trading.

Dwelling on the Markets

Dwelling on the markets and day trading gets you to the point that you are good at reading the markets, reading charts, placing trades, and making profits with your knowledge. Dwelling on day trading is when your mind naturally wonders and ponders all of the subjects that are tied to successful trading.

If you are dwelling on the level of the S&P 500, you might be thinking, "Why did it go up (or down) so much in the past week?" Or you might be thinking, "I have really made a lot day trading that S&P ETF. Why? Did I call it right, or did I get lucky? If I got lucky, should I stop trading and do more thinking of why I was in tune with the markets?" If you are trading oil futures, you might be thinking the same, but you might start to dwell on where the market will be in the fall, when the hurricane season starts. You might be thinking, "The summer was really cool, does this mean the winter will be especially cold? If this is true, how should I be looking at heating oil and natural gas futures? Are the other traders thinking the same thing? Does my broker have any thoughts?"

If you are day trading FX you could be thinking that the European Central bank has been behind in raising interest rates in comparison to the Norges Bank. You should ask yourself, "Does this mean they might raise rates in the near future? Will going long on the EUR/NOK be a good trade after the European Central Bank makes its rate announcement later this month?"

Or you might be planning a trip to Switzerland for the winter holidays and notice that the Swiss franc has really gone up in value compared to the dollar since the last time you checked. Ask yourself, "Why? Is it time to go long on the USD/CHF?"

Day trading what you like will go a long way in your studies and will get you to the point where you are naturally dwelling on the subject of the market, your account, and making money by day trading. Your goal is to get to the point that you think about your account all of the time. This is how you will become an expert at day trading.

Become an Expert

Once you have determined what you would like to trade, you should strive to become an expert on the subject. The best way to become an expert at a subject is to read, listen, watch, and study all you can. This constant reinforcement will get you to the point where you think of day trading enough to always be on the lookout for opportunities to make day trading profitable. Using more than one method will help condition your mind to the idea and subject of day trading.

Becoming an expert is a matter of focus and endurance. It takes time to build upon the knowledge you might bring from your outside life to the day trading table.

It might mean spending extra time wherever you are thinking about the subjects associated with day trading, such as the world's economies, the growth of some of the fast developing Asian countries and how it effects the price of commodities, any sovereign debt problems and how they affect the currency markets, the weather and how it effects grain futures, etc.

QUESTION

Should I take a class in day trading?
Most classes about day trading are taught by companies that would like you to subscribe to an electronic-trading system that they are selling. Your goal should be to develop your own system, know yourself, and know when and what to trade.

Your goal should be to think about how the market is affected by different factors whenever you have a free moment. It is much like a young person in a very competitive college environment, continually studying, reading, and learning. But because a student at a competitive school has developed her ability to assimilate information and concentrate before going to college, she is ready for the challenge, and builds upon her skills. It is not necessary to give yourself quizzes or any other study aids that you would use for preparing for a class; however, there will be a test, and the test is when you are actually day trading with real money. Take your studies and preparation to become an expert as seriously as a college student studying for a final exam.

▼ HOW TO BECOME AN EXPERT

All Sectors	Read brokers' reports, news wires, magazines, newspapers, trade journals; watch TV market news
Gold and Silver Futures or ETFs	Visit bullion dealers to get acquainted with gold and silver bullion, read Kitco.com (*www.kitco.com*), visit the World Gold Council's website often (*www.gold.org)*
Energy Futures, Energy Stocks, and ETFs	Read refinery and oil company websites, notice daily and seasonal change in gasoline prices at the pump, read the U.S. Energy Information Administration website (*www.eia.doe.gov*)
Currency ETFs, FX, Currency Futures	Visit the Bank of International Settlements website (*www.bis.org*) and foreign central banks websites (*www.bis.org/cbanks.htm*)

Many of the sectors have very good websites that feature information as to production, output, estimates, and conditions related to the sector you are trading. Searching through these can yield a broad-based knowledge in the subject.

Knowing Your Markets

In order to make a trade successfully you will need to have your market and sector knowledge developed to the point that you will notice an opportunity immediately. By scanning your resources, checking the charts, and planning, you should be able to enter and exit trades that are profitable. You should only do this when you know so much of your preferred sector and market that you feel something is priced wrong, and offers a good chance to make money trading. Often, this expertise comes about after watching a market for a few weeks to a month, and watching every tick of the charts, even on your off days. You'll develop a very high sensitivity to the market through constant reading and studying of market information, coupled with a monitoring of the charts and daily price changes.

This sensitivity to the market and your sector is how you want to feel when you are trading. You should not have the feeling that you are trading blind; in other words, entering into the market first, and getting a sense of where the market is second. Do not get into this habit. Developing your expertise is a craft in itself. You will need to nurture your market knowledge by giving yourself every chance to study and review the market and your day trading account. For example, you might have your trading platform open but not engage in a day trading session. This would give you a chance to follow the news and relate it to a shorter timeframe chart. By doing this, you'll gain a sense of how a security moves throughout the trading day, all without committing funds to a trade. When you are in the process of developing your expertise, try to link it to what the market is doing on a daily basis. With this technique you will learn to interpret all of the market reports, sector reviews, and entry and exit point market chatter in a daily market price context, not as isolated commentary.

What to Trade if You Work

Depending upon if you are going to be day trading full time or get into it slowly by starting part-time, there are different sectors and markets that are available during different parts of the day. You have many options if you are trading part-time, whether during the morning, mid-day, or evenings. You also have options to trade late into the night, and options for placing trades that carry overnight that you can check in the morning before you go to your full-time job.

E-Mini Futures

If you are trading in the morning, perhaps before you get ready for your job or before getting the kids ready for school, you will find that the futures markets are wide awake and in full trading force. If you are thinking of day trading in this timeframe you could consider day trading any of the **e-mini futures contracts** that are on the exchanges. Most e-mini futures contracts are futures contracts that are structured much like the full-sized contracts, except the e-minis have much smaller lot sizes. Because they have smaller lot sizes, they are easier to manage, and it is easier to have multiple positions in your account at any one time. You might want to trade S&P 500 e-mini contracts, or any of the other U.S. market-based e-mini index contracts. These are good to trade because they have the volume required for good movement in both directions, and with practice, their direction can be followed and predicted by the overnight Asian and European market indexes.

Other possible e-mini futures include energy futures contracts as well as an e-mini gold contract and e-mini silver contract. These e-minis are a good way to get into the world of day trading futures. More information and a full listing of e-minis and other futures contracts can be found on the CME Group website: *www.cmegroup.com*.

The Forex Market

Another idea of what sector to day trade early in the morning is the tried and true Forex market. The mornings in the United States are in fact the busiest trading time for FX worldwide. This is due to the fact that there is a tremendous volume of FX trading in the European markets (particularly the UK), and their trading hours overlap with New York's trading hours at around 4–8 A.M. EST, Monday through Friday. This overlapping of hours can lead to some of the heaviest trading times, and offers a great time to put in some early morning before-work trades. It can be a good feeling to place a few trades, make money in the market, close up shop, and get ready for the rest of your day.

If you are trading FX in the early afternoon (6–9 P.M. EST) you might find that there is very light volume and your trade lacks movement because the Asian markets have not yet fully opened. To compensate for this, extend the expected average holding length of your positions to allow extra time for the trades to develop.

If your mornings aren't free, but you find that you have time in the evenings, you could also trade the futures and FX, but due to the fact that the market is somewhat closed worldwide, volumes will be thin, and there might not be much action, either upward or downward. A bit of volume does pick up after 11 P.M. Eastern, as the Asian markets are getting into full swing during this time, and the Asian currencies including NZD and AUD are traded frequently during these hours.

You could, of course, trade in your FX account in the evening with a **stop-loss** and a **take-profit order** in place at the time of the trade. In this way you would be making an overnight trade, and your trading platform would automatically prevent a big loss and at the same time allow you to realize the profits when the trade moved in your favor. Overnight trades are very popular in the FX market, and include variations such as setting buy-in orders at specific prices along with close-out orders. This would make your whole overnight FX trading 100 percent automated, with you only determining entry and exit prices and letting your trading platform perform the trades for you when the currency pair approached those price targets.

What to Trade Seasonally

Once you start to study the markets and begin trading you will notice that during certain times of the year, different sectors will have more volume and more volatility, both of which are elements to a good day trading environment. You might even notice that some of the sectors have an overall unidirectional movement over a particular season, meaning the sector will trend on average in one direction for that season.

Fall and Winter: Gold and Commodity Currencies

The trading year begins with the fall interest in the markets overall and ends with professional traders all over the world taking their summer vacations. During the fall to spring sessions, it is usually a good time to start to build overall long positions in the gold market, either using gold ETFs or gold futures. This is due to the fact that gold tends to build in price starting with heavy physical gold buying in the fall and ending in the spring. You could also use long exposures to the commodity currencies such as AUD, CAD, and NZD to enhance your long gold positions. These currencies are called **commodity currencies** because they are the currencies of commodity-producing economies. For example, both Australia and Canada are heavy gold producers, and New Zealand is a major producer of soft commodities for Asia.

FACT

Lower-yielding currencies, such as CHF and JPY, are considered safer because their low interest rates indicate that they have less room to depreciate. On the other hand, the high-yielding currencies, such as NZD and AUD, are charging a higher risk premium: they have a greater distance to fall to come in par with the lower yielding currencies.

Fall, Winter, and Spring: Equity Sensitive FX and the S&P

Additionally, the stock markets tend to build interest after the end of the summer vacation months and volume in the month of October. With this in mind, good trades can be made with stocks, S&P 500 futures, and ETFs. Certain currency trades are subject to the following of the stock market's ups and downs. If you are interested in trading the currency markets, you could go short on the U.S. dollar versus the Swedish Krone (USD/SEK) and go long the Australian dollar versus the Japanese yen and the New Zealand dollar versus the U.S. dollar. When the market is falling and there is overall risk aversion, a long exposure in the yen (JPY) or the Swiss franc (CHF) will usually result in gains, as traders flock to the lower-yielding (lower-interest-rates) currencies at this time.

Fall and Spring: Energy

During the fall and spring seasons certain energy trades are in play. In the fall, with the onset of the cold winter months, the energies that are related to heating homes and offices can have good opportunities for trading. Natural gas futures, heating oil futures, and energy company stocks are good sectors to watch. In the spring and into the summer driving months, gasoline and crude oil futures and oil company stocks offer day trading opportunities.

When to Trade the Hot Market

The market usually just chugs along, in a general, lazy upward motion with only the occasional down movement. There are other times that a market, whether equities, a currency, a commodity, or an index is on a roll, and is moving full steam ahead. It is during these times that traders all over the world are on the same side of the trade, and this pushes the price of the sector higher and higher with each day. Markets such as this can only be described as a runaway train, as there is a lot of momentum behind them, and they seem to move in only one direction with no end in sight.

When you are aware of this type of movement in a stock, sector, or index, you have two choices as to what to do. The first is that you can get out of the way: the market is on a roll, is moving forward, and probably will not stop until a bubble is created, and the bubble pops, sending the market back to pre-momentum levels. This is a defensive play, and is a very safe way to not get caught up in the beginning of the creation of a problem in the market. Markets, sectors, and securities can only expand in price for so long, and when they reach the end of their growth, everyone wants out at the same time, causing a lessening in demand and eventual collapse in price.

The secret is to get into the security before the bubble collapses. This is known as getting into the **hot market**. Knowing when to get into the hot market is not as important as knowing when to get out of the hot market, as the top of the pull is never quite signaled until it is too late and the sector has already started to collapse. In a hot market, the best thing is to keep your trades focused in a very short timeframe, and never have a trade on the books longer than one trading session. This means no overnight trades, no carry trades, and no longer-term, accumulation-type trades.

FACT

Bubbles can happen in every market, sector, security, and with every form of good. The seventeenth-century tulip mania in Holland is one good example, as is the U.S. housing bubble of 2008–2009.

This should not cause any less returns, as a hot market moves in one direction rapidly almost every day, often over several months or even a few years. With this in mind, get in and get out with your trades, as you would never want to be the last one in the trade as it started to go down. When a hot market is in a correction stage, that sector should be completely off limits to trading. When the security is going down in price, don't be fooled into thinking that you are doing well and getting a value by buying on the dips as you would in a normal market.

In a collapsing market there are no dips, only lower and lower prices. The sector should be off limits from day trading and position building for a while. This is true because as there are usually many people who made money on the upswing in the price of the sector, there are usually many more that got burned and lost much when the bubble burst. These people remember their pain well, and will be reluctant to get back into that security again for a while—many will never return again. This does not preclude the fact that there are other sectors, securities, and objects to speculate.

A Good Trader Trades It All

Day trading is a way of life. Once you are used to placing trades, waiting for a turnaround, and closing your positions at a profit, you will naturally be thinking of trading everywhere you look. Even though it is not day trading securities, there is a certain element of looking for trading bargains, buying the cheaper end of the trade, and position/cash management in almost every aspect of life. It can be quite fun to take the skills you have honed during your day trading sessions when you are looking for collectables on eBay, buying antique books, or trading in your old car. A good day trader trades it all, from swapping old stamps to buying vintage British motorcycles to making deals at a Paris flea market. This also means that you should carry your talents to other parts of the day trading world, including moving among stocks, ETFs, commodities, and futures. Even within the exotic world of futures there are exotic exotics such as frost futures, cooling futures, and warming futures. There are cocoa, coffee, and credit futures. The FX arena also has its share of exotics, such as the Swiss franc/Hungarian forint cross (CHF/HUF), and crosses that involve the Russian ruble, Chinese yuan, and some of the Baltic currencies.

A good trader trades it all, and is always looking for a new bourse to trade at and use her skills. Keep a look out for new places and new products to trade.

Finding new sectors and securities to trade might mean opening up a new account at a different type of broker and moving some of your trading money to this new firm. This will allow you to gain access to other parts of the day trading world, and will give you new arenas in which to try your skills.

Whatever and wherever your trading takes you, your skills are used the same way. Keep it fresh and interesting. Maybe it means you should begin to deal in rare coins or art. This is, in fact, the way that the patriarch of the famous Rothschild's Bank started his career of trading and banking.

If you are always looking for different sectors and markets to trade in, you will be going a long way in keeping your day trading skills sharp, fresh, and current.

CHAPTER 7

Choosing a Brokerage Firm

Before you actually begin your day trading career you will have to go about the business of choosing a brokerage firm. It helps to think of this selection process much like an interview for a job vacancy you have at your day trading firm. There are the basic interview questions to ask, including can the broker do the job, and does he have the skills to succeed. Lastly, you need to know if the candidate is a good "fit" with your day trading company.

Types of Firms

When choosing a brokerage firm you will have different choices, depending upon the type of sector you are interested in and your opening balance.

▼ **BROKERAGE FIRMS**

Type	Benefit	Disadvantage
Deep-Discount Online Firms	Good for stock and ETFs	Not broker assisted
FX Brokerage Firms	Low account minimums, high margin	Not broker assisted
Multiple-Sector Firms	Low-to-mid account minimum, high margin	Not broker assisted
Combination Firms	Broker assistance when required, multiple sectors	High minimums
Full-Service Firms	Excellent source of trading information, broker assistance for setting up complex trades, multiple sectors	High minimums, high transaction costs

Deep-Discount Online Firms

The first type of brokerage firm you can consider is the **deep-discount firm** that only offers services online. These brokerages will offer a discount on the price if you exceed a certain amount of trades, usually above fifty in a monthly period. If you plan to do Forex trading, be ready for a completely hands-off approach from the brokerage firm. Many do not offer any broker assistance, and often offer only limited technical assistance, if any at all.

FX Brokerage Firms

If you will be day trading in an FX account, you will need to keep very good records of your cash deposits, cash withdrawals, and all of the gains and losses for each trading day. These firms will not send you a statement every month, and will not list the trades you make over the quarter or year. Most likely they will keep track of your overall profit and loss as it accumulates in your account, but often this will roll over from year to year. In this aspect, with the FX accounts and others that do not send you a statement or send you a loosely based one, it is best to keep track of your profits, losses, and interest earned on a daily profit and loss sheet.

Multiple-Sector Brokerage Firms

The lack of records provided by a brokerage firm should not prevent you from considering that brokerage firm if it fits your needs in other matters. Perhaps you would like to be able to trade gold, oil, and FX; in that case you would do well by opening up a **multiple-sector account**. Multi-sector brokerage accounts usually have a higher minimum then the pure FX accounts, as the "lot size" in the other sectors might require a higher minimum to trade effectively. For example, some brokerage firms offer full multi-sector accounts with 200:1 margin with an opening deposit of $2,500. Again, with this type of account you would not get any type of broker assistance in setting up trades, and you would not get any type of statement from the firm.

You can keep track of your daily net gains, losses, and interest earned using pre-printed paper trading forms. These forms also have places to record the stock index levels and overall market conditions present during that day. They can be used for tax purposes and to have a permanent record of your trading successes.

Combination Brokerage Firms

Combination brokerage firms have trained licensed brokers available to assist in the setting up of a trade or a hedge trade. They have two types of pricing structures, one for online trading at the discount rate, and one for broker-assisted trades, at a higher, full-service rate. This higher rate can be worth the price if you are just starting out, setting up a complicated trade, or would just like to "talk through" the logic of a trade before making a commitment to it.

Full-Service Brokerage Firms

The inclusion of a full-service brokerage firm will help out greatly, even though the high commissions will prevent you from day trading in this type of account. The research and education supplements provided by full-service firms are indispensable in your day trading career. They offer overall market technical analysis, sector and industry-specific analysis and information regarding the trading potential of the S&P 500, ETFs, commodities, and currencies as to where to place enter and exit points during your trading day. Although most of the brokerage firms will give you access to some kind of news feeds and research reports, some of the reports are nothing more than a collection of articles that are on the public access news sites such as CNN or Forbes. The key is to get access to the best research and day trading ideas that you can, even if you have to pay for it. The way around this is to open an account at a full-service brokerage firm that offers insight into the markets you are trading in their offerings. Perhaps you can put your "other" money into this account, roll over your 401k, open an IRA, or retail brokerage account with your investments, long-term money, or mortgage, in some cases. The yearly price the full-service brokerage firms charge to keep the account open can be anywhere from $75–$250 a year, but the benefits of having access to all their reports and information is worth the price.

FACT

Foreign currency brokers usually charge very low commissions on popular pairs, called majors. Higher commissions are charged on other currency pairs, or crosses, consisting of two major currencies paired less commonly. The highest commissions are charged on infrequently traded pairs, referred to as exotics.

Commissions and Fees

Since the costs of the commissions and brokerage fees are subtracted from your overall profit, it makes sense to try to get the lowest fees possible for each round trip of trading. Some commissions are a flat rate, and can be as low as a few dollars a trade (with a trader's package) at a deep-discount firm. Some firms have a sliding scale, with a discount pricing schedule for self-directed trades and a different pricing structure for broker-assisted trades. Futures brokers are usually set up in a way to be combination firms. Again, with the combination brokerages, you could ask advice as to how to buy different product that might have the effect of hedging the trades you will be making during that trading day or for the next few days.

Don't look to your broker to give you advice as to how to manage your account. Brokers will shy away from telling you what to do to make money. It is best to remember that it is your money, your trade, and your decision as to how to day trade. Never give anyone else responsibility over your account.

FX trading accounts base their pricing in a different way. They usually have a set percentage of the currency amount of the currency pairs posted in their commission structure. The commission is deducted automatically from your trade balance after the trade is placed, with the net effect of putting you at a loss at the moment of the trade. The commission is based upon 1/100ths of a percent, often referred to as **basis points**. These basis points commissions are called **pips**, i.e., each basis point is a pip. The pip price that you will pay for your trade will stay the same regardless of the size of the trade. In other words, if the commission structure for a EUR/USD trade is 1 pip and you place a trade of 10,000 EUR/USD, the commission will be 1 EUR for the round trip of the trade. If you place a trade for 1 million EUR/USD, the commission will be 100 EUR for one complete opening and closing of the trade.

Advantages of Certain Accounts

There is a real advantage to having some sort of assistance when you need it. While the brokers at combination firms usually do not offer advice as to what to buy in order to make a profit, they can set a trade up for you that you might otherwise have trouble setting up yourself. For example, you know that the trading you are going to be doing for the next few days will tend to be "risk averse" in nature, i.e. you are going to be short the S&P, long gold, and long the Japanese yen. In order to slow down some of the movement and dampen wild swings in your account, you could hedge against the risk averse positioning in your trading portfolio.

Your discount brokerage firm might switch into full service mode and guide you; your broker might suggest a combination of small positions that would be structured to gain in value if the market started to take a more risky stance. Since the Swiss franc (CHF) is considered less risky (and moves up when there is less appetite for risk), the broker might place a short CHF position with a stop-loss order to prevent any dramatic loss in value to the downside. The positions will make money when the market goes down, and these two net positions have the potential to have the effect of lessening the impact of a really big movement in prices in the wrong direction against you.

Disadvantages of Some Accounts

One of the disadvantages with certain brokerage accounts is the method in which you get money into and out of the account. Some accounts are quite easy to set up, and need only proof of residency, proof of citizenship, and a bank reference. After you have your account set up, you will have to fund it; this can be a problem as some brokerage accounts only accept one form of funding and liquidation. For example, once the account is opened, you will choose the way in which you will be funding the account: PayPal, debit card, wire, or check.

If you are in a hurry to fund the account and begin trading, or starting with a small amount, you might deposit your money into your account with a PayPal deposit or debit card. This process is usually smooth and efficient, and the money can be credited to your account quickly. An advantage to this method is the fact that the funds can be credited after banking hours; this can be a real help if you are trading late and you would like to put more money into your account within that trading session.

Since you will be funding your account with PayPal or a debit card, your deposit will be less a service charge by PayPal or the debit card, a fee of around 3.5 percent. This fee can really add up when you are dealing with larger amounts, and effectively will put you at a loss even before you start to trade.

Some brokers require account liquidations to be the exact method of account funding. Accounts funded by check, wire, credit card, or PayPal will be liquidated in only that same way. This is important when you are planning to make bi-weekly or monthly withdrawals from your account as a salary draw.

Your bank might charge a fee for sending funds to your account via federal wire. Fees for outgoing wires can range anywhere from $35–$75 per wire. Outgoing wires are usually only processed in the beginning of the day, Monday through Friday. This account funding method will work especially well if you are sending larger amounts, as the fees associated with the wire are fixed regardless of the fund amount, acting as a volume discount. With fed wires, a deposit is considered "good funds," meaning you can trade with them usually at the moment of the deposit, with no need for them to clear.

The slowest method of all is to send a check. This traditional method costs only the price of a postage stamp, and can be a happy medium between the cost associated with wires and alternative funding methods such as PayPal and debit card. You will have to plan when and how much you will be sending, as it will take until the check arrives and clears before you can trade with those funds.

Types of Accounts

Regular accounts usually only allow you to trade stocks and ETFs. These accounts do not allow trading on margin, meaning you will only have the buying power of your cash balance. Regular accounts are good for beginners, because the lack of a margin limits position size and risk. Additionally, you will be limited to **long-only trades**, a trade where the stock or ETF gains in value when the price of the stock or ETF goes up in value. You can get around this not having the ability to have a short position by building a position in ETFs that are "bears." A bear ETF will go up in value when the basket of stocks it holds will go down: the ETF is structured in a way as to be a short position and be using margin internally. This is a really effective way to gain exposure to the short side of the Dow 30, S&P 500, and foreign indexes. There are also bear ETFs with a focus on industry sectors such as energy stocks, gold mining stocks, and financial/banking stocks.

The best way to gain experience with bear ETFs is to buy bear ETFs in your demo account after a few days of big gains in the market. Keep track of the percentage movements of the ETF when the market reverses, as it will take some time to get used to the inverted nature of the gains.

Leveraged ETFs

The second way to simulate margin in a regular account is to use a leveraged ETF. These ETFs are internally structured in such a way as to offer 1.5x, 2x, or even 3x leverage of the underlying basket of stocks in the ETF. Since the leverage is built in, you are able to buy these ETFs in your regular account. They are priced in such a way to reflect the leverage in the ETF and will move up or down at 1.5x, 2x, or 3x the rate of the underlying product in the ETF. This can lead to some spectacular gains, as market movement is really amplified by the internal margin.

Additionally, there is no risk of a margin call and no threat of going past zero in value. A **margin call** would happen if you used the margin in your account like a credit card to purchase the ETF and the value of the position fell far enough to require you to either close out the position and pay back the margin you borrowed, or have the option of depositing more money in your account to be above the required amount. Margin calls are looked upon as unfavorable and can be very disruptive to trading—automatic closing out of your position can destroy your cash balance without the opportunity for the trade to turn around.

Margin Accounts

Margin accounts are where you put in a certain amount of cash and the brokerage firm supplies you with a credit card–like balance that is able to give you additional buying power—some margin amounts are limited by regulation, such as stocks and futures.

Margin amounts can change during volatile times in the market. For example, regulators often change the amount of margin requirements in the futures market. This is done to slow the amount of movement in the market when the volume or volatility is excessively high. This modifying the margin requirements in trader's accounts has the effect of cooling the market, as there is less cash and buying power in the market for speculators.

It is required that you have a margin account if you would like to short stocks and ETFs, or trade FX, commodities, or futures. Margin amounts can range from one half to 500x your position size. With this added buying power you can make profitable trades with smaller account balances. You can do very well with a $25,000–$50,000 cash balance in your account in a stock or futures account and a $2,500–$5,000 cash balance in a 50x–500x margin account in FX. You will need to take extra care with concentrated positions and use risk-management techniques to limit losses when using margin, as profits and losses happen quicker than in a regular account. The use of the pyramid method in building your positions, managed position size, and diversification across industries, commodity types, and currency, will also help in limiting your exposure to risk.

Is This Broker Good for You?

There are a few things to look for when evaluating whether or not to open an account with a brokerage firm. You should look at all of the benefits that having an account at that firm would offer:

- Is the account setup easy to understand?
- What is the account minimum?
- Are the commissions reasonable?
- What is the available margin?

- Is the margin amount adjustable?
- What sectors can you trade with the account?
- Does the brokerage firm offer free demo accounts?
- What is the quality and ease of use of the trading platform?
- What is the quality of the research and news-feed services?
- What is the quality of the technical support?

You should also be looking for a broker that has the option of having a daily newsletter or market news updates sent to your e-mail account. This option will give you the ability to keep on top of your overnight positions and any other market developments that would affect your trading. Your goal should be to have enough flexibility to enjoy time away from your trading desk without being worried about adverse market developments.

With this in mind, there are some brokerage firms that have secondary trading platforms with simplified order-entry systems that allow the buying and selling of positions from handheld Internet connections available through smart phones. The combination of up-to-the-minute reports, market news, and simplified access can give you a complete account-monitoring system for when you are away from the office, but want to trade.

Other Considerations

Other things to consider when choosing a broker are the quality of the training and trading support. Training can be offered at a local office or online, and after speaking with a live broker you should be able to determine if trades are explained well, if hedging techniques are offered, and the option of talking through trades and market conditions. Lastly, questions should be asked as to if there are any monthly fees on top of the commissions and whether or not there are any account inactivity fees for when you are away from trading temporarily.

Your cash and securities purchases will be handled through your broker's back office. Where and how your cash balances are deposited and how your securities purchases and sales are handled relate to the administration of your account. Here are some questions to ask about a firm's administrative practices:

- Is the partner bank that holds your cash deposit highly rated?
- Does the broker pay a reasonable amount of interest on your unused balance?
- Can you place the unused portion of your account balance in a high-yielding CD?
- Does the account compound interest daily?
- Does the account compound interest in carry trades (FX accounts)?
- Is the interest offered in the carry trades competitive?
- Is it possible to enter in pending orders when the market is closed?

The final question to ask is if it is possible to open an account in a currency other than U.S. dollars. This option is valuable if you are making frequent trades in securities that have the second currency as a component.

When shopping for a broker, don't make it your goal to go with a brokerage firm that offers the lowest commissions. The old adage "you get what you pay for" is good to remember, as brokers with a little higher commission structure can offer a lot higher-quality day trading experience.

For example, if you trade foreign exchange futures or FX, you can get a more favorable commission if the base currency is the same as the currency pair: AUD to AUD/JPY or CHF to EUR/CHF, as opposed to USD translating to the base of the currency pair first. With this arrangement, it is important to know the exchange rate of the initial foreign base currency funding and the interest rate offered on unused balances.

CHAPTER 8

How to Navigate the Online World of Day Trading

When day trading, you will need to learn how to keep a short-term and long-term perspective. You will also need to learn how to use day trading software to get account information in relation to your open orders and your profits for the day. Lastly, it is very beneficial if you can use a practice account. It will help you become smooth with your order-entry skills and have a place to try out new trading strategies and ideas.

Short-Term and Long-Term Perspectives

You should keep your analytical perspectives in two time buckets: short term and long term. Your **short-term perspective** should be ultra-short, and only be the time it takes to evaluate the day's market conditions and news, look for setups, and commit to a trade. This short-term perspective will then last until the trade is closed out and reviewed. You should be thinking of each trade with a short-term perspective. These short-term trading elements include cash and margin amounts, initial and pyramiding position sizes, price-of-entry points, and the overall risk level of the trade.

ESSENTIAL

Fifteen second, thirty second, and one minute charts will help you get a short-term timeframe perspective. Ultra-short timeframe five second charts will let you see each trade as the security moves up and down in the market, but do not show enough perspective of the overall market.

With a general overview of the fundamental market conditions, you should place a trade with the thought that you will be committed to the idea only as long as it takes to make a profit and close out the trade.

ELEMENTS OF THE SHORT-TERM PERSPECTIVE:

- Daily evaluations of overall market conditions
- Immediate evaluations of available cash and margin amounts
- Scouting for individual trading ideas
- Evaluation of the risk element of a potential trade
- The use of ultra-short-term timeframe technical charts

Short-term timeframes last from a few minutes to a few days depending on the holding time of the trade. You can have several short-term perspectives as you buy, sell, and hold many different positions during your trading day. Each one of the trades is alive when it is open, and the risk will not go away until you close it out. If you keep short-term perspectives on each trade, you will be evaluating each trade on its own merit apart from the longer-term perspectives that helped you evaluate the market in the first place. If you use the long-term perspective to guide you, but use the short-term perspective to evaluate each trade when you are in one, the combined effect will go a long way in keeping your day trading profitable.

Long-term perspectives usually involve timeframes of three to six months and rely heavily upon fundamental analysis as well as technical chart evaluations. This combination can lead to very convincing arguments as to overall market and trading conditions for a particular sector. For example, your broker might issue a report that trading in commodities will be profitable in the next six months but especially in the energy sector. You could then evaluate the potential for each energy futures, energy stock, and energy ETF trade with this overall perspective. It would also work out well if you included this sector in your daily review of market conditions in an effort to build up knowledge and familiarity of energy securities. You will then be able to use this sector knowledge, and a long-term perspective will help you evaluate potential trades with a short-term perspective.

A long-term perspective also includes macro knowledge of the overall world's economies and market conditions. These are the really big picture ideas: sovereign debt levels, currency strength, and the role of the world's developing economies are some of the subjects associated with a long-term perspective. These subjects take time to learn, and don't often change that quickly. Again, country, market, and sector fundamentals are taken into account along with fifteen minute, one hour, and one day timeframe technical charts (a one day timeframe chart might show the price movement history for the past two or three years).

What Software Tells Traders

Your trading platform should provide you with the basic account information, access to news reports, and access to charts with different timeframes. Elements of a trading platform's account information should have cash and trading information, including:

- Balance in the account
- Margin available
- Margin used

- Unrealized profit and loss
- Realized profit and loss
- All open trades
- Number of units in trade
- Profit and loss percentages per individual open trade
- Price purchased and current price of each trade

You might also see news reports coming across the news wire in one part of your screen, and of course, the price boxes of your watched securities—the flickering from green to red as the security moves up and down in price.

While most day trading can be done with a laptop and one computer screen, investment-banking, proprietary traders often use a two-screen setup. Other independent proprietary trading firms use as many as eight screens at a time to keep track of each day trader's positions!

If you look at the activity section, you will see a history of your account including cash deposits, in and out trades, and daily interest payments (if your account has them). As you build up trades during the trading day, the open trades will show on the trades section where you can watch them go from the initial purchase into a profit zone as the market moves. If you have four, six, or more positions open, you can close them out one by one as they become profitable by opening up the close order box and waiting for the last possible moment to realize your gains. The gains will then be added to your balance, to your realized profit and loss, and to your buying power for the next round of trading.

With your account software you can quickly look at your open positions and see what trades are in profit and which ones are in loss. You can also use the charts to track an open position and get a graphic representation of your trade as it moves up and down. With this method you will be able to see your entry point marked on the chart. You can also draw a line on the chart to mark a point that will be your selling point. The graphic charts showing your trade as it creeps into a profit trade will give you a good idea of how the market is moving for that trading day.

Also, when you have built a hedged position, and your hedge has worked well, your trading software will tell you the overall net trade profit in percentages and dollar amount. When this happens you will be able to close out all of the components of the hedged trades with one click, allowing you to lock in the profits of the trade. Your software will then allow you to review the hedged trade for quality and effectiveness, as it is always important to see why a trade worked well and what can be improved.

The Benefits of Practice Accounts

You will do well if you have a brokerage account that allows the opening of a practice account or demo account for your use, as these accounts have the same software and order-entry system as the live accounts. Your demo account will be off the books, will be funded with imaginary money, and all profits and losses will be on paper. These accounts can be very beneficial in giving you the opportunity to try out different leverage amounts, improve your order-entry skills, and allow you to try trading in different markets and sectors that you might not have experience with. You can also use the practice account to develop a disciplined investment technique, and give yourself a chance to get used to trading and experiencing your reactions to the market's ups and downs without risking actual money.

When you use your demo account to place a trade that is according to your broker's recommendation, you can monitor it over time, in an effort to prove the quality of your broker's advice. You can use a demo account to try out your own investment hunches, and use it to trade when it would otherwise be an inappropriate time to trade. For example, it might not be a good time to trade when the market is especially volatile, when there are uncertainties as to where the market is going, or when the risk levels associated with day trading are inappropriate to your personal situation.

Gains in a practice account will still make you feel very happy, especially when you win a big trade after interpreting the markets on your own, or when you plan out a hedge and it works in the way you planned. Overall, the use of practice accounts can go a long way in building day trading skills, gaining confidence, and keeping your account intact by giving you a way of trading during inappropriate market conditions.

ALERT

Make sure your brokerage firm offers a practice account that remains active during the whole time you have a live account open. Some brokerage firms offer demo accounts that are open for only a month and then automatically close. These practice accounts have to be reopened every month.

Getting Smooth with Order Entry

Before you begin to trade with real money, you will need to become very smooth and confident with the order-entry system on your trading platform. You would not want to be worried about making a mistake in a trade; e.g., long instead of short, wrong dollar amounts, wrong number of units, wrong stop levels. Practice will also improve your finesse and confidence for closing out a trade when you need to, whether at a profit or a loss.

It is in your best interest to practice your trading platform's order entry and order closing many times while using your demo account.

Start your order-placing training with **scalping** (trading using a five to ten minute timeframe), and using small sums of money. Before each trade, write down the security or FX pairs and margin amounts you are going to use on paper before you place the order. This will give you time to think through the trade. You can make a decision as to go long or short as you see the market going. Don't worry about doing it very quickly at first, as speed will develop with practice.

An Example Trade

For example, you could see that the overnight Asian and European markets have performed well. You could decide to go long (buy) 100 shares of a 3x S&P 500 ETF in an effort to capture the gains you think will be in the American markets. You would determine ahead of time that you would like to make a 5 percent profit out of the trade. After planning out the trade on paper, you would go into your demo account and set the trade up in the order-entry system of the trading platform. You would double-check your order, and then execute (place the trade).

Emotions can run high during a typical day trading session. A lot of stress can be involved with trading large sums of money in an active and moving market. Use your demo account to get familiar with the high-pressure world of day trading without the risk of losing real money.

To learn the quick order-entry skills required for day trading, you should immediately open the close order box and monitor the profit/loss level until profit is shown in the trade. If the market is moving slowly or there is time until the 5 percent profit comes, take your profit early, before your profit goal is met. Your goal is to just get the feeling of making a round-trip trade.

More Beginner's Tips

Trading in and out in a few minutes with just a little bit of profit will go a long way in giving you skills and confidence. The key is to build on profitable trades to develop positive experiences going into and out of the market. Stick to one trade at a time, with round lots of 100 shares, 1,000 units of FX, etc., as it is best to develop skills one at a time. When you get used to round lots, you will think in terms of percentage profits with those trading numbers.

If the demo account offers a large sum to practice with (such as $100,000 or $250,000), don't overuse the account, as this will color your expectations as to dollar profit amounts. If you overuse the account and get used to placing big trades, you will get discouraged when you begin trading with an amount that is less than the amount in your demo account. It is best to trade a few rounds and take a break, as it is really easy to get tired when you are trying to learn this new skill. It is also human nature to get fatigued with making smaller trades for a long time and want to make one big trade for the day and quit. Resist this temptation, as this will not help you. Learning to trade is like learning a foreign language: It is better to have shorter learning sessions every day than to have one or two long sessions infrequently.

How to Try Out Ideas

It's very helpful to have a way to try out new strategies and ideas without trading in your live account. Keep a strategy notebook as a place to write down and plan your trading ideas. For example, keep track of:

- Overall market conditions
- Day, time, month, season
- Level of the U.S., European, and Asian market indexes
- Price of oil
- Price of gold
- The level of a commodity index
- The price of the major currency pairs

FACT

Professional money managers and investment advisors at the world's major investment banks still use a paper-based method of keeping track of their client's positions. Even though there are many software packages that can help you with the notes and recording trading ideas, there is something to be said about keeping a paper journal of your day trading activity.

Use your notebook to write down your strategy and its source. For example, you could write, "Merrill Lynch advises to accumulate long exposure to NZD/USD at anything below 69." You would write that today it is at 66, the market has been down for the past three days. The Asian markets were up 1.5 percent overnight and now the European markets are up 0.5 percent. Thinking that you would like to try out the theory that the U.S. markets will follow when they open, you decide that a long NZD/USD position will be a good trade. After writing down all of the facts to the setup, you then place the trade in the demo account.

This trade will be separate from all other trades that you have going on in the demo account. With this trade, you must be extremely professional and cool headed about the execution and strategy. For example, if the trade turns out wrong, you should let it ride until it corrects, checking it three or four times a day. When you monitor it, make marks as to the market conditions, such as "the S&P went down for a fourth day," etc. Do not modify the trade, change stops, or add to the trade in any way.

What you are learning is how to spot setups using theory and how to build confidence by seeing a trade to the end. If there is an unannounced, unpredictable event such as a natural or manmade disaster or unannounced economic statement, then you should cancel out of the trade and void the experiment, as these things were not in the variables of the original trade experiment. You can have several experiments going on in your demo accounts, and they work best when there is emotional involvement with the success of the trade. If you plan, observe and act in a cool, calm, and professional manner, you can learn a great deal. Keep track of the trade, and when the experiment is finished, take notes as to time in its development, market conditions that developed, and the profit that was made.

Paper Profits, Real Emotions

Trading in your demo account will give you the greatest benefit when you feel the full emotions of winning and losing at day trading. When you are trading in your demo account you will be experiencing the ups and downs of the markets, the thrill of the order entry, and the emotions related to profits and losses. It is important to feel the full emotions of success and failure, as this is one of the keys to learning how to be successful in day trading.

You will learn how to spot setups, how to manage your cash and margin amounts, and how to use a risk-management program such as the pyramid process. When you are using the full educational benefits of a practice account, you will learn how to resist the temptation to close out of a losing trade because you are angry, when to take your profits without getting greedy, how to use moving stops (by using automatic trade closeouts to lock in profits), and when to take a loss. It is important to experience the full feelings of "ruling the markets" and "knowing everything" when you have a series of profitable trades, as well as experiencing taking on too much risk in search of more and more thrills.

It's all right to have losing trades in your demo account. Every day trader should experience placing too big of a trade and losing in a big way. It is better to have paper losses and have feelings of "I should have" with play money than to feel the pain in real dollars.

The more you can learn in the demo account, the better trader you'll be. Consider your demo account as lessons learned cheaply. In this way, you should take care of your demo account as you would a regular account: use care in the trades you are placing in it. Take a lot of ownership and pride in your demo account and build it up over time, just like you would a real account, as it is a measure of your developing day trading skills.

CHAPTER 9

Listening to the Market

You will grow skills in looking for day trading ideas by listening to the market. There are different sources of information for getting information about the market. How much information, the source of the information, and the quality of the information are some of the questions you should be asking whenever you hear or read a report on the markets. Whether it is from your broker, TV, or the Internet, you should ask the question, "Does this information help me decide what, when, and how much to day trade?"

How Much Information Should You Listen To?

When you are looking for trading ideas, what you really want are situations in which the market has priced the stock, currency, or commodity too low or too high. In other words, the market has temporarily oversold or overbought the product, and during the short term (the trading cycle), there is a good chance that other traders will react. This reaction by other traders to a mispricing causes markets to reverse, even if only slightly. You should be thinking in the immediate short term when evaluating day trading situations. Look for opportunities in which you can place a trade that will gain momentum in your direction, with the intent of then getting out of it as soon as it makes a profit.

There are many sources of information to help you interpret the market's levels and determine entry and exit points. In the beginning you learn what sector to day trade, when is a good time to place and order, and at what price to place the trade. To get a big picture of the market, you should read and listen to as much information as possible.

Granted, some information may be biased, sensationalized, or common knowledge, but it is a good idea to begin each day trading session by accessing at least four to five sources of information before you place your first trade. This will get you into the mindset required for a successful day of day trading.

When you read or listen to market and economic reports, keep in mind that you are not only looking for facts as to what sectors and prices you are going to be trading, but you will also be determining what the other day traders and the other market participants are thinking. Consider it intelligence gathering (by looking into the other team's play book) to get into the right frame of mind when watching TV business shows, listening to radio shows that report on the market, and reading Internet forums. Remember, these are public sources of information and should be treated as a general insight into the market, not as a determiner as to your day trading activity.

You should be referring to your broker's reports and daily newsletters as well as looking at your five minute, one minute, and thirty second charts for today's day trading entry and exit points. It is really important to go into each session with a big picture and general overview of what sectors will be in play during the day. Base each and every commitment of cash and margin on your individual interpretation of your trusted sources along with technical interpretations using short timeframe charts.

When you begin each day trading session in a top-down approach (listening to the news, reading the reports, looking at long timeframe charts, switching to short timeframe charts), you will get into the market's mood very quickly. If you have an idea that a stock, FX pair, or future will move, sit back and watch the short timeframe chart move up and down with each buy and sell order. You will be able to notice a slight creeping into one general direction and with the general big picture of the market and that sector, and be able to confidently begin placing trades into the market.

Where to Get Information for Trading Ideas

While there are many places to look for trading ideas, most importantly you should be looking at two places: trusted sources and market chatter. Trusted sources will tell you the direction in which the market is likely to be going in the future. These are usually the longer timeframe reports and market summaries that are published by your broker. Market reports and summaries offer a logical view of the market. They are often based on mathematics, past market activity, market fundamentals, and technical indicators. These longer reports should be read during times when you are not trading. In your off hours, you should study them for content and absorb the themes the analysts are presenting. For example, the report might say that there should be a "more cautious stance taken in the market overall for the next few weeks." You might learn that the S&P 500 has entered into an overbought range. This means that according to fundamentals, the stocks in it have an overall high average **P/E (price/earnings ratio)**, meaning the prices of the stocks are too high compared to the estimated earnings of the companies. Also, the report might state that the S&P 500 has been sitting near a **resistance level** for a week, unable to breach an important level.

With these two pieces of information, the report summarized that the S&P 500 is near its top and will be there for a while. In fact, it might enter into a stall, or worse, a correction (when an overvalued market is sold off to more realistic levels).

Brokerages are known to cater to either individual day traders or to institutional day traders. Firms focused on individual day traders will offer more explanations in their reports, both on the fundamental and technical sides. They have a more education-minded goal than the institutional-focused firms. Look for samples of a firm's reports to determine its bias.

You would know from this information that it is a good time to have a short positioning in the market, i.e., the market has a good chance to move down in the next month and you would like to capture this movement.

Market Chatter

The next place you can look for ideas is the short-term news reports, commonly called **market chatter**. The key with short-term news reports is to use them to outsmart the markets. Remember, there are a lot of people reading the same reports and reading the same charts, and the market moves in a herd mentality. You will have to decide, from your overall knowledge and what the long-term reports tell you, if the point at which the price of the product is overbought, oversold, or neutral. It best to use the short-term public indicators, such as the wire reports with buy and sell points, as an indication as to what most day traders will be thinking. There is a good chance that day traders everywhere have the same buy and sell points in their mind: They are all reading the same charts and short-term news reports. Because of this, never enter your trades on the guidance of these reports. It is better to use them as an intelligence gathering and as a look into the ideas of the other market participants.

Information versus Noise

With finance, the markets, and day trading, there are a lot of people telling you what's best for you and what you should do. It is good to remember this because market movement prediction and economics are not absolute sciences, and there can be a lot of different ideas and opinions as to what's the best view of the market.

> Brokerage firms are known to place tremendous pressure on their brokers to get clients. Some firms have training programs that have quotas of $1 million a month in new, investable assets over a two-year period. These brokers will be very eager to land your account. You should proceed with caution when dealing with these types of firms.

Learn to be choosy as to whom you will accept as your information source. You will naturally think of economics and the market all of the time when the market is really hot and you are trading day in and day out. Your goal should be to get yourself to the point where you are the expert, hearing all information sources and opinions as noise. Even though you still might read the *Wall Street Journal*, watch CNBC, and consult your broker's reports, you must get to the point when you are scanning for a key bit of information that you can use as a trading idea.

Considering Emotions

Remember, you are dealing with the markets: most information sources deal in facts and logic, but the market is one of the most illogical "animals." This is because all of the investors and traders are dealing with money; along with this money comes emotions of fear and greed. The herd mentality, coupled with the fact that most players in the market are, in a way, placing educated bets, leads to emotional and illogical markets. It helps to think like a professional gambler, with the markets as your huge, worldwide casino. The casino of the markets has so many variables that it is foolish to think that an information source can predict them all. This is what the big quantitative hedge funds and trading desks of investment banks attempt to do: the application of logic, statistics, and mathematics to unpredictable markets that are driven by emotion. When you think of yourself as truly an independent day trader you will pull yourself away from the information and view it as all noise, all chatter, but also an inside view as to what the other market players are thinking and feeling.

Can You Believe What You Hear?

It helps to think of yourself as your own client: You are in business and you are your only customer. If you were a contractor building a house and the house was your shelter (and the house is your financial well being) you would need to hire subcontractors that specialize in certain aspects of the building project. You might hire a plumber and an electrician, making sure that the plumber and the electrician were the highest quality and most experienced that you could find. When you went to the lumber yard to get wood for the construction, would you listen to the people in the store telling stories of when they installed a sink or hung a ceiling fan?

How do you evaluate the motivation of a market commentator?
Market commentators are required by regulation to reveal if they or any of their clients have positions in the security they are giving an opinion on: a clear notice of their benefit from the comments.

Would you listen to your mechanic discuss the time he had a concrete driveway poured and the contractor used the wrong mix? Wouldn't you be very selective of the sources of information in regard to your construction business? This is how you have to think about accepting the information that is out there regarding the stock market, oil, gold, interest rates, currencies, or the economy. People everywhere love to talk about money: they love to talk about how much they have, how much they don't have, the killing they made, and how much they lost in the market. Everyone with money has an opinion, as money can be very democratic as far as profits and losses are concerned.

Questions to Consider

When you hear someone talking about the market (or money in general) ask yourself, what is the motivation? Is the person on the news really convinced that what he is saying is true, or is he just making a statement to fill time on the air? Is the article in the magazine really that important, or does that magazine need to have that many pages and the publisher fills it with fluff? Is this person overall negative in nature because he had a bad experience, and does this mean you will have the same experience? How much of the report you are reading is based upon fact? Can this be true? What is the researcher's track record? Should you or shouldn't you care what the market thinks? Remember, if you were a contactor buying supplies and hiring subcontractors for your building project, would you take any plan that was given to you? Would you pick up wood and nails off of the street, even if they were free for the taking? Would you ask a dentist to approve the quality of your supplies? The best thing to remember is that it's your money. Have confidence with your views, and be selective with the information you believe.

By nature, TV news and Internet feeds have to have stories to fill the minutes and hours of the trading day. Even on the slowest, most uneventful trading days these news stations and Internet sites will deliver news with a heightened state of energy, which can make the information seem somehow more important than it really is.

Internet Forums and TV

Two types of information sources have the ability to change the content of their information products very quickly: Internet forums and TV. Both have the ability to change what they include in their news stories as the news happens. In this way, Internet forums (whether news feeds, chat rooms, or market-recommendation sites) and TV can be very reactionary to the market's news as it develops. They are very good at this capacity, and if used to get information on the rapid developments in the markets, it is acceptable to follow them. Their writing and reporting style has a tendency to be sensationalized, and small developments in the market are looked upon as big stories.

It is good to remember that the Internet forums and TV are regarded as being wide and shallow in their reporting. This means that they have the tendency to report on any and all blips on the information radar, but the reporting will consist of small sound bites and one or two written paragraph blurbs.

You can use Internet forums and TV in your training as to how the markets and some of the aspects of the economy work. It is best, however, to use them almost as a form of entertainment: listening to the newscasters and reporters as storytellers who monitor the emotions of the market. Make sure you do not look at TV and Internet forums as true, fully informed sources of recommendations to your day trading activities. Better yet, do not base your decisions to buy or sell any security on these types of information sources. In this regard, there are stories of financial advisors at the big full-service wealth management firms telling clients to turn off CNBC when the market goes through a particularly volatile trading day.

Good or Evil: The Market and "News Days"

Your first and foremost goal in day trading should be capital preservation with capital gains as a secondary goal. This means that you should always view each trading day and each trade with the mindset that a cash position is the safest place to be, and that you will only enter into a trade if there is a reasonable expectation of a capital gain. You should manage your risk to preserve your capital and only take measured risks in relation to the potential gain of a trade.

With capital preservation as your primary goal, you should enter into trades with thoughts that the market will react and move in the future in a way that can be predicted with some degree of certainty. For example, you think that typically the S&P 500 trends in one direction for two to three days and then reverses. You can make a reasonable assumption that if the S&P 500 has been up dramatically for three days straight, then it (and the other risk-sensitive trades, USD/SEK, AUD/JPY, AUD/USD, NZD/USD) will be ready for some of the market participants to sell off some of their holdings, and engage in what is called **profit taking**. You also might have observed that when there has been a multi-day run up in the market with big gains at the end of the week, traders will often relish their gains over the weekend and sell on Monday to lock in their good fortunes. With this in mind you could short the market, buy a bear S&P ETF, or build a position in risk averse currencies.

When the primary goal of your account is to make capital gains, you will be forced to take risks with every trading situation. It would be unacceptable to sit out a day, and it wouldn't be acceptable to forgo a series of risky trades in favor of ending the day with nothing more than interest earned.

Economic News Days

The problem comes with economic news days. Economic reports are held in great secrecy before they are announced. Brokerage firms, TV news commentaries, and Internet forums will have predictions and statements as to what the market thinks the report will say. Often, when the economic report comes out and it is different as to what the market expected, there will be a reaction: The market will move up or down according to how accurate the market predicted the news. On the other hand, if the report comes out and the market predicted it exactly right, the market often has already **priced in** what they expected. In other words, they built the expected positive or negative news into the value of their trades and positions. When this happens, the market will sell off anyway, as the event is then in the past, everyone knows the actual numbers, and profit taking will take place. Trading during the various news days, whether news from the United States, Europe, or Asia, can be very tricky due to the fact that the outcomes can't be predicted with reasonable accuracy. News days should be avoided with the idea of capital preservation being your primary goal. The markets will always be there; you can always trade after the news comes out. It is best not to have any positions in your account leading up to the announcements, especially if the positions are directly related to the sector that the news reports are relating.

CHAPTER 10

Reading the Fundamentals

Reading the fundamentals is the process of knowing the economic or financial statements of a country, market, sector, or security. Financial statements can tell you how well a company is doing; you'll need to look for information on a company's structure, EPS (earning per share), and P/E to give you these clues. You'll also have to analyze the supply and demand of commodities, and the fundamentals of the world's economies and currencies. Lastly, you'll have to know the shortfalls of using fundamentals as a tool to predict a security's future price.

Knowing the Company or Sector

When you are first starting out in the process of learning how to **read the fundamentals**, it will be important to find and read as many sources of information as to the country, market, sector, or security as possible. This is how you really get to know the product you are going to day trade. You should by no means skimp out in your readings when it comes to fundamental analysis. The fundamentals of a country can be found by performing an Internet search for the central bank and/or national bank of that country.

Links to the world's central banks can also be found on the Bank of International Settlement's website: *www.bis.org*. Read through the documents and cross-reference them with the information provided by your broker. Some brokers provide a semiannual report of different regions of the world economy. These are also excellent places to find a bird's eye view of the economy and investing (trading) outlook of some of the world's countries.

If you are thinking about or are currently day trading a company or sector, you can sign up to receive RSS feeds about the security as news is reported. Some independent news services also offer this service. Signing up can be as simple as filling out a form and providing your e-mail address.

Your broker can also be a source for a market overview, and can often produce a monthly sector guide as well. Full-service firms do especially well at this, but some of the independent discount brokers use the piggy back method of offering the research of a full-service firm they are in association with. Individual firm's literature, 10-Ks, past **annual reports**, and press releases can be found on a company's website, and are really good sources when looking for specific information, such as a company's cash flows, balance sheet, etc. Individual companies and sector's research reports written by your broker, online conference calls sponsored by companies, and online conference calls sponsored by the different departments of your brokerage firms (FX, equities, commodities, etc.) are also excellent sources of the information required for you to begin performing a fundamental analysis of a security.

Looking at Financial Statements

When looking at financial statements, begin with the **annual report**. In the annual report you will find the **letter to stockholders**, which tells you how the company has been doing and where they would like to go in the future. The **letter to shareholders** also tells the nature of the business operation. The **income statement** shows sales, expenses, and net income; this is shown over a twelve-month period. The **balance sheet** shows cash, what is owed to the company (accounts receivable), and fixed assets.

Fixed assets include equipment, buildings, land, vehicles; they also show the value of any intellectual property such as patents, the value of trademarks, and lastly any intangible assets, such as the value of goodwill. Goodwill is the value that the business puts on the **synergy of the business**—the synergy of the business is how their customers are better served by the company operating as a whole unit, as well as the value of their repeat customers. **Liabilities** are also shown, and these are the short-term and long-term debts of the company.

How do you know that a company is being truthful in their financials?

All public companies are required by regulation to have their books audited by a licensed CPA firm. Companies usually take great pride when an auditor gives their stamp of approval on a set of financial documents. There are exceptions to the rule, such as the financial misconduct of Enron that came to light in 2001–2002.

The last thing that is shown is the **stockholder's equity**. The stockholder's equity is a representation of the difference between what the company owns and what it owes. The last statement is the **statement of cash flows**. The statement of cash flows shows how money flowed in, out, and through the company during the same year as the income statement. The statement of cash flows shows how the company sourced the cash needed for its internal growth: It shows whether the cash was internally generated through sales during the normal course of business, through the sale of an asset, or through the raising of cash through the sale of debt or equity stakes in the business.

Structure, EPS, P/E, and Growth

Capitalization is the sum of the long-term debt and the stock in the set up of the company. This is often called the structure of the company, and the amount of debt in relation to the amount of equity in the company will tell you how conservatively the company is structured; the lower the amount of debt, the more conservative. This is because during a slow economy (when sales might be off and the company does not produce as much cash), there is, in proportion, less debt to service. Therefore the company can make fewer payments toward its debt and use more to pay for other things to keep the company running.

FACT

The capital structure of a company is usually carefully planned. In fact, there is thought to be a perfect balance between debt and equity on a company's balance sheet. The formula used to find this optimal mix is called the **weighted average cost of capital**. The WACC varies upon the cost of debt and the tax bracket of the corporation.

This also means that if they keep the level of debt down, they will have a greater chance of being able to service the debt they already have. This will keep the company having a high credit rating; when a company keeps a high credit rating they can get lower rates on their debt in the future. This leads to even lower debt service payment, making the company even healthier. Cash flow is an analysis of the cash flow statement and will tell you if the company is financing their growth from their own generated sales, from the sale of assets, or from raising money externally.

Of course, the best way a company can raise money is from its own operations, which are the company's normal course of business. This would be determined from the "cash flows from operations" sections of the cash flow statement. The other sections would tell you if the cash for the company was generated from the sale of assets, under the cash flows from investing. If the company is selling off assets to raise cash or produce a profit, this should be looked upon unfavorably, because what happens when the company does not have any more assets to sell? A company should be providing the majority of their cash flows from operations if the company wants to have a sustainable business.

Earnings Per Share and P/E Ratios

Earnings per share, or **EPS**, is found by taking the net earnings and dividing it by the total number of shares outstanding. If a company had $10 million in earnings and the number of shares is 1 miilion, the EPS would be 10. Another method of looking at the price of a stock or ETF is the P/E ratio. The P/E ratio is the price of the stock divided by its earnings. P/E ratios can tell you how expensive a stock or ETF is compared to others in the investment universe. The lower the number, the cheaper the stock, and if a stock has a higher than usual P/E numbers, this might be an indicator that the stock has crept up in value in relation to others in its industry sector. It may also indicate that it is a good time to short the stock because, all things being equal, companies in the same industrial sector usually have close to the same P/E ratio. When one is out of whack from the others, this usually means that that stock or ETF is undervalued or overvalued compared to the others in its class.

Measuring Sales Growth

Another method of determining if a company is doing well is measuring its sales growth. The sales growth of a company can be found by looking at the sales of the previous three to five years. There should be clear indications as to a growing sales base: there should definitely not be shrinking sales numbers. This would be an indication that something was wrong with the product or management of the company.

The Supply and Demand of Commodities

Commodities often move higher when the equities market is stagnant. From the mid 1960s to the early 1980s, stock markets all over the world did not increase in value, but commodities did very well during these times. Unlike equities and equity futures, commodities have a limited supply. The supply is in a glut when the world's economies are doing poorly, and the supply is tight when the world's economies are doing well. Developing countries, such as China and India, use enormous amounts of raw materials in their ever-growing industrial sectors. China has the most demand; they have demand for soft commodities, grains, and industrial metals. China and India also have a large appetite for gold, as this is often a preferred store of wealth for the people who live in these countries.

While the supplies of commodities are limited and inelastic, the world's supply of money is ever changing. The supply of money moves up and down according to the actions of the central banks and treasuries of nations across the world. When there are excessively lower interest rates in a country, this usually signals a large supply of money.

Oil is in limited supply and it is difficult to discover new sources of this commodity. Oil is used by almost the whole world, as nations rely on oil in the progress of their economies. Natural gas is used to heat homes and process products throughout the world; it is difficult to source natural gas, and difficult to get it to its end user. Metals are in high demand and include copper, silver, iron, as well as other industrial metals. In fact, demand is so high for some metals that there is a significant scrap industry, such as the iron and steel scrap industries that make shipments to China. The grains and soft commodities include corn, sugar, and others; these are renewable, but demand increases when the world's economies are growing quickly.

Commodities of the Past and Present

In the 1980s and 1990s there was a slowing in the demand for commodities, and this led to a bear market and lessening of prices overall. Commodities are now considered inexpensive, and the 1980s and 1990s bear market caused a lessening in the production capacities of those producing commodities. This will potentially cause a steep supply/demand ratio as the world's economies start expanding at full force. This is because commodities are fixed in supply and the world's money supply is ever expanding. The ever-expanding money supply will force a supply-and-demand imbalance, as there will be more dollars, yen, and euro chasing the same or fewer amounts of commodities. This will lead to a steady upward pressure in the price of commodities. Due to the fact that most commodities are now traded electronically in the futures markets, there are very few barriers to entry, and professional money managers, commodity hedgers for companies, and speculators can get into the business of commodity trading worldwide with just an Internet connection. The commodities market is truly a worldwide market, and knows no borders. The commodities market can potentially be a very good place to set up shop, and can lead to very profitable day trading sessions for those who are willing to master the fundamentals of this area of trading.

Currency Fundamentals

Most currencies use the **floating rate system**. The floating rate system means that the exchange rates are not set; however, they might have a target amount set by the central bank of the country or economic entity that issues them. In general, currencies are allowed to float up and down against the values of other currencies as dictated by market forces.

In some cases, the governments or central banks will attempt to regulate the value of their currencies through the practice of **intervening in the markets**. This is done by the government or central bank buying or selling its own currency in the inter-bank market in an attempt to force a change in value of that currency.

If the central bank would like to increase the value of their currency, it would sell off their foreign currency reserves and use the proceeds to buy their home currency. This action would push up the price of the home currency while pushing down the price of the foreign currency. If the country would like to make their currency go down in value, the central bank would increase their amount of foreign currency reserves by buying currency in the open market with their home currency. This would increase the amount of the home currency in relation to the foreign currency, and the effect would be to lower the price of the currency. This is referred to as quantitative easing, and was done heavily by the Swiss National Bank after the 2008–2009 worldwide banking crisis. This event, and others related to it, caused the Swiss franc, commonly known as the "Swissy" or CHF, to rapidly and dramatically rise in value against other currencies, including the euro and the U.S. dollar.

Since the "Swissy" gained so much against Switzerland's trading partners, Swiss exports were stunted, and the Swiss economy began to slow. Remember, if a country relies on exports for its GNP (gross national product), then it will help the country's economy when the price of the currency is low against its export partners. As this exchange rate will make the home country's exports cheaper for the importer, the importer will buy more of the exporter's cheaper goods, giving a boost to the exporter's economy. A similar situation is happening in China, where the price of the Chinese yuan was pegged to the U.S. dollar at a rate that could not be sustained in relation to all of the exporting that China was doing with the United States. The currency is now beginning to be revalued and is appreciating against the U.S. dollar.

With the **Bretton Woods system**, the U.S. dollar was linked to gold. Foreign nations could easily exchange the dollars they had in reserve for the gold that was held in the vaults of the U.S. government. When Bretton Woods ended in the early 1970s, the dollar was no longer convertible to gold, and with this, the "gold window" was closed.

It is often very difficult to determine if a country's currency is overvalued or undervalued against another; the currency markets tend to oscillate between overvalued and undervalued with timeframes that range anywhere from several months to several years.

Using Purchasing Power Parity

A good method that is often used to determine if a country's currency is over- or undervalued is called **purchasing power parity**, or **PPP**. PPP is a measurement of the misevaluation of the same goods from country to country as measured in a base currency, such as the U.S. dollar. This PPP level is also known as the **Big Mac Index**, a term coined by the publishers of the periodical *The Economist. The Economist* publishes their version of a PPP measurement by recording the cost of a McDonald's Big Mac in several countries around the world. The thought is that the Big Mac is a good measure of PPP, as it is the same commodity worldwide. If the price of a Big Mac is higher in one country than another, then that country's currency is usually overvalued against the currency of the country that sells the less expensive Big Mac.

Although there are some problems with the ability of fundamental analysis to predict a securities movement in the future, it serves a key starting point in the analysis of the markets in general. While some disagree to its usefulness, none can completely disregard its function when studying the economy.

The Problems with the Fundamentals

While using fundamental analysis is an excellent starting point for building a case as to whether or not to build up a position in a security, there are some fundamental flaws. First, the information that was used in the building of the financial analysis might not be 100 percent correct, or it may even be outdated. Second, some of the key numbers used in the analysis of the security might be off, such as a company's estimated growth rate, or the estimate of a country's PPP. Lastly, even though the information related to the fundamentals and the numbers used in the estimates are true and correct, there might be a delay as to when the market reacts to this information. The combination of this misinformation, inaccurate estimates, and market delay can lead to a situation where you are building a well thought out position in a security and the trade fails to turn a profit or materialize in the way that you intended.

Analysis Promotes Success

Granted, there are some basic flaws in fundamental analysis. Even though the threat of these flaws is real, the process of fundamental analysis is often a key element in a well-thought-out day trading campaign.

Reading the fundamentals, searching for trading ideas, and then switching to reading the charts in an effort to look for setups is the hallmark of a quality day trading business. This process of starting with the big picture, looking at a country's economy, a particular sector, a security, and then switching to technical analysis to make the final decision as to a possible entry and exit point is often referred to as a **top-down approach**. This top-down approach is used by the largest and most successful investment banks and hedge funds in their pursuit of outstanding risk adjusted returns. It leads them, and can lead you, to a more focused security selection all the while enhancing your returns while providing a method of allowing a form of intelligence-based risk management.

If you can get the hang of reading the fundamentals, you have gone a long way in increasing the enjoyment and profitability of your day trading endeavors.

CHAPTER 11

Adding Charts to Market Analysis

The analysis of securities wouldn't be complete without the analysis of the technical indicators. Bar charts, Elliott waves, and moving average deviations also have a hand in helping you analyze the markets, look for setups, and identify the entry and exit points of a trade. Some of the indicators tell a story about the entire market, while others are sector or security specific. The addition of technical analysis to the study of the fundamentals can result in a powerful trading program.

Security Timing Approach

While fundamental analysis looks at economic data, technical analysis looks at the supply and demand data as presented by indicators. Technical analysis can be used for forecasting, and if used in conjunction with fundamental analysis, you can have a very successful day trading business. In fact, the big investment banks use both methods, and this is often called the top- down approach. When you are looking at the big picture and using fundamentals, you are using a **security-selection approach**. But when you are using charts, you are using a **security-timing approach**.

A chart of a security represents a snapshot of the securities price and volume over time. The most useful chart is called the bar chart. You can find access to a securities bar chart on your day trading software or at any one of the commercially available sites on the Internet. One of the best sources of charts and technical information is Big Charts found at *http://bigcharts.marketwatch.com*.

Some day trading platforms allow you to call up charts and draw trend lines directly on the chart. When this software is available, it is often possible to place your cursor right at the point you would like to make a buy or sell order. This can help you get a visualization of where your trades are on the chart.

Charts can be adjustable as to the timeframe they cover. In order to get a full background viewpoint you could look at a weekly chart, which shows the securities closing prices at week end. These weekly charts usually show a history of a year or longer, and are good for getting a perspective of the price history of the security. For day trading purposes you could switch to hourly and fifteen minute charts, to get an up-close look at the movement of the security in a shorter time interval.

Bar charts show the closing, the highest and the lowest price of the session. They also include the volume of the security during that session. Volume is a good indicator when you are looking for support and resistance levels, and breakout activity.

Chart Patterns and Dow Theory

Patterns appear in a bar chart over time and each pattern offers different types of information. Support and resistance patterns show traders the psychology of a security's price. When you draw a line at the average bottom price and top price you come up with the **support and resistance of the security**. The top line is called the support level or support line. A breakout is when the security moves above the support level. When a break out is reached, there will be added excitement in that security, and if the breakout is reached with above average volume, this indicates the formation of a new trend.

The resistance is the bottom line, and when the security gets to this point, traders will sell out of the security. If there is a lot of volume at the support or resistance, this means that there are a lot of traders using this as entry and exit points. When a security travels past its support or resistance point with a lot of volume, it is thought to be a good breakout. The point of the breakout is called a **pivot point**, and is often followed by a test of the breakout, a time when the market rethinks the breakout, and the security falls in price.

> There is often much activity when a security reaches a support or resistance level. This is true because day traders all over the world have drawn the same lines. Many of them have come to the same conclusions as to where those important levels are, and are ready to react when a level is reached.

Having an ascending triangle or descending triangle is when you draw a line along the top supports and along the resistances. If the lines make a wedge shape then there is a good chance that there will be a breakout in that direction. A gap occurs if the trading of a security opens above or below the close of the session before, this is often due to the market's reaction to overnight news.

Dow Theory is used to plot the future movement of a security using the Dow Jones industrial 30 average and the Dow Jones transportation averages as base lines. There are hourly, daily, and weekly movements in the market, and when these converge in the Dow Jones 30 and then are confirmed when the Dow Jones transportation averages reports the same trends. This theory has been around for many years and many technical analysts still use it.

Elliott Wave and Moving Average Deviation

The **Elliott Wave Theory** employs past information of a security movement to predict the securities future direction. The basis of the Elliott Wave Theory is that securities in the market have five distinct steps, and these steps form three separate waves. The theory is that once all of the five parts of the different parts of the wave have worked their way through, a top (or bottom) is in play. When a top or bottom is reached, this also marks the beginning of a fresh trend. There are flaws to the theory, and they are similar to the flaws of the Dow Theory, as there is no distinct separation of the different steps, and it is often difficult to determine a step's number in relation to the others; i.e., you might be thinking a step is number four in a series when in actuality it is number three or even number two. It can be difficult to decipher the elements of the Elliott Wave Theory accurately. This should not, however, prevent you in determining for yourself its value, as many professional traders rely on its indicators in their day trading strategies.

Don't be too concerned with your calculation of some of the indicators. Often, indicators such as a 200-day moving average can be easily drawn with some of the software programs that are available. Once an indicator is drawn on a chart, the chart can be saved and refreshed at each trading session.

Forty-Week Moving Average

Many technicians refer to a securities price in relation to its forty-week moving average. The forty-week moving average number for a security is figured out by taking the security's ending price for the previous forty weeks and dividing by forty. The next week would be added to the initial number, and the first week of the group would be dropped. This results in a forty-week moving average, and this has the effect of smoothing the picture of the securities closing prices. Forty-week moving averages are also known as a 200-day moving average.

Fifty-Day Moving Average

Another useful chart to look at is a security fifty-day moving average. The measure of a security's rate of movement is called its **momentum**, and is measured by a security's **moving average deviation**. This number is calculated by dividing the security's last price by its ten-week moving average. Many professional day traders use this method to analyze securities that have a tendency to be very volatile. This indicator can help you determine when a new trend is in play, when a security is overbought (too high), or oversold (too low). Ten-week, or fifty-day moving averages are also useful in helping you get a longer-term perspective.

The Stochastic

Another useful indicator is often referred to as a security's **Stochastic**. This is the measurement in percentage terms of the price velocity of an individual security or market index as compared to a range set by a technician. The higher the percentage of the Stochastic, the closer that security's price is in relation to the preset range. A Stochastic of 0 percent would indicate it is at the bottom, while a Stochastic of 100 percent would indicate that the security or index was at the top of the range.

Other Charts, Technical Indicators, and Money Supply

The popular periodical *Investor's Business Daily* publishes the relative strength number for securities. The relative strength of a security is designed to measure a security's relative price change in the year prior and compares it to all other securities. A relative strength number of eighty and above is considered exceptional.

Japanese Candlestick Charts

Japanese candlestick charts are read much like bar charts. The main difference with a Japanese candlestick chart is what is reported on the chart. The high and low for the day, and the opening and closing price of the day are shown. Also, there is a difference in the charts for when the end of the day price is lower than the beginning of the day price, and vice versa. There are many terms that go with the formations that Japanese candlestick charts make; there is also a general consensus with many professional traders that Japanese candlestick charts are inherently too complicated for any serious use.

If you find a charting system, ratio, or indicator too complicated, too difficult, or too hard to understand, feel free to switch to a chart system or indicator you feel comfortable with. Day trading is difficult enough, and you shouldn't feel obligated to complicate it further.

Technical Indicators

Technical indicators are a day trader's best friend. Even though not every indicator works every time, there are so many that do work reliably that the study of several can have a combined effect of being very valuable. Technical indicators are drawn from business information, investor activity, market activity, etc. Keep in mind that with technical indicators it is best to use several at once, and if they are all telling the same story, then you can consider the information as good.

Money Supply

The first technical indicators involve money supply. Money supply is literally a measure of the amount of money that is in circulation, and includes both paper and electronic forms of money. It can represent the cash in circulation, the amount in checking and savings, and the amount in commercial paper—often referred to as M1, M2, and M3, with the lowest M number representing the most basic form of money: cash in circulation.

When money supply increases through an expansionary regime of a country's treasury or central bank, there is literally more money available for people to use to buy things with. One of the things people have a tendency to buy when there is more money available is securities. A study in the sixty years following World War II proved that security prices go up when there is an expansionary money supply. The money supply indicator is calculated monthly, and shows a year over year percentage increase or decrease. This number is adjusted for the Consumer Price Index, which has the effect of taking into account the impact of inflation.

The **money supply indicator** is calculated by starting with 100 and adding the percent change in M2, and subtracting the percent change in the Consumer Price Index. The resulting number gives that month's money supply indicator. If the number is under 100, that means that the rate of the money supply is less than that of inflation. In this situation, equities historically have remained flat during these times. If the situation was reversed and the money supply indicator was over 100, equities would generally do well, as has been historically shown.

More Indicators

The relative value of the market as a whole can be measured by comparing the ratio of the S&P 500 average earnings per share to the percentage yield of a ninety-day U.S. government T-bill. This indicator is called the earnings per share/T-bill yield ratio, and can be calculated by dividing the twelve-month earnings per share for the index by the average price of the index. The next step is to take this number and divide it by the current yield of the ninety-day T-bill. The rule of thumb is when the EPS/T-bill yield ratio is above 1.19, it is considered an indicator to buy equities. When the ratio is below .91, it is time to sell equities.

Another indicator is called the **short interest indicator**. Markets across the United States usually make a statement in the middle of each month reporting on the amount of short interest. This report shows the amount of shares that are held on the short sale side of investors and traders. Not only does this number represent how many people are in the mindset that the stock market will go down, it also shows the amount of buying power the market has at the time. It is reported in a ratio or the short interest over the average daily volume of the market. An indicator below 1.0 is considered a bearish indicator, and a ratio of 2.0 or higher has historically been considered an indicator to buy equities.

Don't get caught up in using only one or two indicators in your technical analysis of the markets or securities. It is best to instead use a handful of indicators along with bar charts and fundamental analysis to reach your conclusions of the market.

The WST Ratio

The **WST ratio** is an indicator that uses information derived from options traders. Options are contracts that give the holder the opportunity to buy or sell at a given price. Unlike futures, options do not have to be exercised, and many expire worthless. **Options' trading** is often considered the most risky form of trading due to the time element of the options. This time element means that as the days progress toward the expiration date of an options contract, they are worth less and less, to the point of having zero time value, only intrinsic value.

The WST ratio is a measure of index option activity. When the ratio is below 38.0, option buyers who expect to make money when the index goes up are outnumbering the opposite traders, and the market is considered bullish. Traders who are looking to make money when the index goes down are more dominant when the ratio is above 62.0. A ratio of above 62.0 would indicate a bearish market. Due to the rapid trading in options and the short holding time of most positions, the WST ratio is an indicator that experts use with only a three-days-in-the-future timeframe.

The CBOE Volatility Index

Another measure of the trader's nervousness and subsequent market sensitivity is the **CBOE Volatility Index**, also known as the **VIX Index**. It is an intraday index and has its main use as an indicator of traders' and investors' emotional feelings about the market. The higher the VIX number is, the greater the negative feelings in the market. A normal reading is anywhere from fifteen to twenty-five. During the worst trading days of the banking crisis of 2008–2009, the number jumped as high as eighty, showing a very high degree of emotional turmoil and even panic in the markets.

Market Breadth, Oscillators, and Others

The **Arms Index** attempts to read the conditions of the stock market by looking at the number of shares on the NYSE that have fallen and risen and the volume of these shares. A number of less than 1.0 tells the story that there are a lot of buyers, and a number greater than 1.0 indicates there are a lot of sellers in the market. A more accurate reading of this indicator is to use the ten-day moving average of the Arms Index.

What do overbought and oversold mean?
When technical analysts refer to a security as being overbought, it usually refers to the fact that the security has risen in price too quickly, and runs the chance of falling in price in the near future. The opposite is true for oversold; the security has fallen too quickly and will soon rebound.

The **McClellan Overbought/Oversold Oscillator** can be helpful in determining the risk of the market. It measures the velocity of the money moving into and out of the markets, and is calculated for the NYSE and the NASDAQ. Charting software can help you calculate this number as a required element is the thirty-nine-day exponential moving average and the nineteen-day exponential moving average. A McClellan Oscillator number higher than seventy-five indicates an overbought market and a reading of less than seventy-five shows an oversold condition. The higher the reading is, the higher the potential of rapid upward movements in price. Very low readings indicate the bottom of a market.

There are other indicators, such as odd-lot indicators, cash holding of mutual funds, the margin amounts of retail customer's accounts, and the insider buying and selling of stock by company executives.

If you start with a top-down approach and use fundamental analysis to select a country, market, sector, and then security, you can couple this information with technical analysis. Technical analysis involves reading the charts, whether bar charts or Japanese candlesticks, and adds to it the reading and interpretation of technical indicators. If by grouping several technical indicators together, you come upon what seems to be a trend, and the charts and the fundamentals are all telling the same thing, then you have discovered entry and exit points in the market. The combination of analysis, cash management, risk management, and controlling your emotions will go a long way in keeping your day trading business fun and profitable.

CHAPTER 12

Cash and Margin Management

Before you begin trading you will need to have the right mindset in thinking of your day trading account as a cash account. After you understand that this cash account can be used offensively and defensively, and how to strengthen it, the next step is the proper use of a margin account. Learning the mathematics of margin, the use of margin, your account's buying power, and the possibilities of margin calls will complete your understanding of cash and margin management.

Your Trading Account as a Cash Account

You should have the primary objective of your trading account be capital preservation. With this in mind, you should be thinking about your trading account as a cash account. This means that your account should be in cash all the time, with you buying a security only when the situation presents itself, and then returning to cash. You should prefer to be in cash, and not want to be in a trade, due to the fact that being in a trade offers the opportunity for risk. This opportunity for risk is the same thing as offering the opportunity of losing money.

If the objective is to be in cash, then each trade would be viewed as a supplement to the normal interest rates that you would earn in the account. When you are in 100 percent cash, you are 100 percent safe, and you will be earning interest. If you are earning an interest rate of 2.5 percent a year on a $50,000 balance, your balance would be $1,250 a year, or about $6.25 per trading day with no risk. If you were accepting no risk, you would have the mindset of thinking of adding to this daily accrual with as little an amount of risk as possible.

The world's largest hedge funds think of their cash accounts in a different way: All of the cash they have in their accounts is invested in 100 percent U.S. government T-bills. In a separate account, they typically borrow against the T-bill deposit at a ratio of 4:1. This 4x leverage is amplified even higher when they day trade FX, futures, and commodities.

Granted, you have to take on a measured amount of risk while you are entering a trade, but if you approach the trading day with the thought that you will be adding to the $6.25 risk free accrual, you will have the appropriate risk appetite for day trading. Remember, the cash in your account is what you will be using as a draw for your salary. In other words, your paycheck from the trading account will be in dollars, and you will be paying your bills associated with the operating of your day trading business in dollars; this is the balance that you should be looking to keep high. You wouldn't want to load up your account in things other than dollars (stocks, FX, futures, etc.) for too long of a time because you eventually have to convert these into dollars to spend on the expenses of the account.

Trading as a Source of Income

Remember, you are in the business of day trading to make money to pay for your expenses, buy the extras you want in life, and add to your overall net worth. When you think about always having to at sometime convert the balance in your trading account back into money (dollars) that is usable for things that are other than securities, such as mortgage payments, car purchases, and living expenses, you will always be thinking of your trading account as a source of income and a cash account that has the ability to be drawn upon at any time to pay for your expenses. When you are always thinking of your trading account as a way of being able to pay for your expenses and to get you to the next trading day, you will not run out of money (dollars needed to pay your bills). If you allow yourself to get to the point where you run out of money you will be forced to close shop and take a job: proper cash account management can prevent this from happening.

The Defensive and Offensive Cash Account

You should be thinking of your cash account in two terms: defensively and offensively.

The **defensive cash account** is the mindset that your cash account is the source of your paycheck and the source of a day trading business's self sufficiency. You should get to the point that your day trading business is completely self-sufficient and in no way harms your total picture of economic well being.

While you might be taking a lower paycheck as a draw from your account in the beginning while you build up your account, you should be thinking of your trading account as a cash account that has a balance big enough to get you to the next trading day. That is your ultimate goal: to get to the next trading day. A defensive mindset will pay the bills associated with trading out of the account with as small an amount of withdrawals as possible. This means that not only will you be day trading part-time while building up your account, you might switch to working part-time before building up to full-time trading. All the while you should keep your cash withdrawals to a minimum by keeping your expenses associated with your day trading business low.

If you have a full-service broker, they will most likely ask you the question, what is this account's primary objective? Even though your primary objective should be capital preservation, you should answer this question with "capital appreciation." This will notify your broker as to what type of advice you will be expecting from them.

An **offensive cash account** is a philosophy of entering and exiting trades with the thought of increasing net worth, no matter how small the gain might be. You would enter into trades and exit trades with the thought of building enough capital gains in your account on a daily, weekly, and monthly average, so that you would be able to have a net gain to pay for your expenses, draw a salary, and better your overall financial position. You would be using both short-term and long-term perspectives to aggressively search for enough trades throughout the week and month to meet your minimum gain requirement, plus an acceptable profit.

Thinking Offensively and Defensively

It is best to think of your cash account in both defensive and offensive ways, often changing perspectives throughout the day as the trading conditions change. You might be offensive in the very early morning hours as you trade S&P 500 futures, and switch to a completely defensive mode after your profit has been made, or after a situation such as when the U.S. markets open and become erratic in movement.

You will get very good with switching between philosophies, defensive to offensive as the situation allows, and as the opportunities to make money day trading in the market change from moment to moment. Remember, you don't always have to be day trading in every situation. In fact, if you have been playing your cash account the right way defensively and offensively, you could choose to sit out trading days when it is not very clear you will make a profit. This way, your account would be able to have enough profit and gains built into it to allow for a day off. Remember, you are looking for weekly and monthly average gains; averaging gains will prevent you from forcing yourself to trade in every market condition.

Strengthening Your Cash Account Through Trading

Most importantly, you must think of any loss that occurs in your day trading account as a withdrawal from the account—e.g., if you have a balance of $10,000 in your account and you make a monthly expense account withdrawal of $500 to pay for the expenses that are directly related to a month's day trading activity, and the same day you lose $500 in your account, you have then made a "withdrawal" from your day trading account of $1,000 for the day.

To bring the account back up to the original buying power of the account, you will then have to make an additional $1,000 in profits to get the account back up to $50,000. This sounds simple, but when you think about strengthening your cash account, you should think of always returning the balance to the original amount at the minimum. In other words, you should be making each month equal to the expenses associated with trading and making up any losses you have incurred, plus an acceptable interest rate.

This is not as hard as it sounds, especially if you take a defensive approach to withdrawals by minimizing your expenses and only entering into trades that you have a very good chance of exiting out of with the same amount you entered with or better.

Keeping the Account Intact

You should be always thinking of keeping your cash account intact. With this in mind, you should enter into each and every trade with the idea that that trade will enhance your cash position, much like a boost of interest. Your cash account doesn't just strengthen with increases; it strengthens with security and potential.

For example, if you have a large enough balance in your account, you might be able to limit the size of the margin you are using on each trade to get into a trade that has a longer timeframe to wait to make a profit on it. With these types of trades, the opportunity to make money might be very evident, if both of the fundamentals and the technical indicators are telling you that the trade is good. There is still a risk involved with the trade, due to the holding length of the trade.

The returns of your account are the combined interest accrual, and the added boost of trading gains is the true measure of your accounts performance. This combined number is often called a **total return strategy**. A total return strategy is used when you have FX carry trades.

You could think of your account in three groupings: the super safe, the risky trade, and the very risky trade. The super safe is your cash balance and the ultrashort-term, small positions that you will close the order on very quickly. These trades are going to strengthen your cash account the most, but do not think of these ultrashort-term micro trades as adding to your balance in terms of generating enough profit to draw against. You are better off thinking about the profit generated from these small trades not as future withdrawals from the account, but as adding to the buying power of your account through compounding and increased margin availability.

This works because if you enter into trades during the trading day that are safe and quick, your profit will add to your purchasing power with compounding when you are using margin.

For every $10 you make in profit by trading one of these lower-risk trades, you will strengthen your cash account to the tune of between $15–$5,000 worth of buying power, depending upon the margin amounts you are using (1.5:1 for equities and up to 500:1 for FX).

What Is Margin and Your Buying Power?

When you have your day trading account set up with the ability to use margin, what you are really saying is that you have to the ability to put up cash and securities as collateral in a loan to buy more securities. Margin is much like making a down payment on a purchase of something tangible, such as a car. With the car, you would put down a required amount and finance the rest. With a car it is often 10 percent down and financing 90 percent, and with a house you put down 20 percent and finance 80 percent.

When you are financing stock, futures, or FX with margin, you are putting down anywhere from 66 percent to 2 percent (or less) of the total amount of securities purchased. For example, you would need to put down $660 for each $1,000 worth of stock or ETFs purchased, and $20 for each $1,000 worth of FX purchased at a 50:1 margin in a Forex account. This loan between you and your brokerage house gets opened and closed with each round trip of securities trading. In this way, your available margin will be going up and down depending upon how many and how large of trades you have open during your day, and will be constantly adjusting to the amount available as you open and close trades.

What margin level should I use when I am trading?
When starting out it can be easier to use a lower margin ratio with your trades, e.g., it lowers the impact of a fast market. You could, however, set your margin level at the point that you would use it normally, and get trained from the start to think about and place trades with higher leverage.

There will also be movement up and down as to the margin available in your account, as the trades that are open move up and down in profit and loss dollar amounts. This cash plus margin amount equals the buying power of your account. The buying power would be added to and subtracted from with each gain and loss of each trade, as well as with each open and closed trade. Because day trading is dynamic in nature with your trades being highly leveraged, the margin and buying power in your account will be moving quite rapidly as each position gains and loses, and is opened and closed.

The Mathematics of Margin

Since margin acts as a multiplier effect on the upward and downward movement of each security through the gain and loss percentages, it is really important to understand the mathematics of how margin works to amplify gains and losses of each trade.

First, set the amount of margin you would like to use. If you would like to use 50 percent margin on a 100-share purchase of a stock ETF, you would need to pay for it with two-thirds down and the other one-third with margin. If the initial purchase was $15,000, you would need to have $10,000 cash and $5,000 margin available.

Let's say that the market was having a really good day, and that the ETF that you bought was up 10 percent or a gain of $1,500. Your actual percentage gain would be much higher than 10 percent. It would be calculated by dividing the dollar gain by the actual amount invested, e.g. $1,500/$10,000, which would result in a 15 percent profit on actual capital invested. This is an illustration of the multiplier effect of the margin on profits.

Adjust the level of margin you use in a trade to fit the amount of risk associated with that security. For example, you know that the S&P 500 has lower volatility; use higher amounts of leverage for these positions. Other sectors, such as the financial sector are very volatile; use lower amounts of margin to reduce risk.

The same dramatic amplification can be shown on losses, as the mathematics of margin works to the downside as well. In the same example, you would put up $10,000 in cash and use $5,000 in margin to come to a balance of $15,000 worth of the stock ETF. If the market was in a particularly bad day, and the sector you were trading was going to the downside of 10 percent, your losses would be amplified much like when there were gains. To calculate the losses, you would divide the loss amount by the total actual capital investment, or $1,500/$10,000, or a loss of 15 percent. The use of margin acts as a lever to increase the percentage movement in the stock, ETF, currency, or future.

Margin Limits

The maximum amount of margin that you are able to use in your brokerage account will be limited by the type of security you are day trading. **Market regulators** are the ones who are in control as to what amount of margin is able to be used in stock, ETF, and futures accounts. This is due to the fact that some of the world's worst economic problems were brought about by over speculation in the financial markets. Over speculation often causes what is referred to as a **bubble in the market**, or a condition of securities that are greatly overpriced due to ease of credit, allowing greater and greater price expansion in the market.

The problem of overheated markets and market bubbles has its roots throughout history. Market bubbles and their subsequent collapse in price have involved a great number of objects of speculation, and have taken place in many different countries. For example, the Dutch speculated on the price of rare tulip bulbs in the 1700s, the English speculated on Joint-Stock companies in the 1800s, and the whole world suffered during the Great Depression, which was exasperated by speculation in the world's stock markets in the 1920s.

The U.S. real estate bubble is the latest of the bubbles that were driven by overleveraging and speculation. Market regulators attempt to control the formation of bubbles by regulating the amount of leverage allowed in trading securities. On the low side, regulators allow 1.5:1 margin. The high side of the amount of margin allowed is the unregulated Forex markets, in which the amount of margin allowable in an account can range from 10:1 to 500:1.

Margin Call

What happens if you have used margin to buy a security and the security has fallen so far in value that you are underwater in the equity you have in the trade? In other words, what if you have highly leveraged the purchase of an FX pair, have used much of your available margin to buy it, and losses put you in a position where you are below the minimum equity in the trade? When this happens, your broker will issue a margin call.

A margin call is when you are given a notice that you will have to put up more capital (usually cash) in order to get the equity in your position high enough to meet the minimum. Some brokers allow you until the end of the trading day to fund the account, while others begin to systematically sell off parts of your portfolio in order to meet the margin. Others immediately close out the position when it meets a level that is below the minimum.

Often a margin call comes when you are not monitoring your positions, such as when you are away from your computer, during an overnight trade, or during an otherwise unwatched longer timeframe trade. If you are making these types of trades, keep an extra cushion of available margin in your account.

In any case, a margin call can be disruptive to your trading, either by requiring you to deposit more capital or by the positions closing. It can be especially costly when a position is closed out without notice, as this takes out all capital involved in the trade and doesn't allow for enough time for the position to turn around and move into a profitable stance. Margin calls can be prevented by cautious use of high margin ratios and active position-size management, such as the **pyramid method**.

The pyramid method is a method of building positions in groups of one third at a time and closing out of the positions at one-third at a time. This is done to average in your cost and selling prices to lock in gains, and prevent a large position being established at an unfavorable price.

Other methods to prevent margin calls include the **2 percent rule**, a method of building in stop-loss settings (automatic closing of a position) to limit the overall loss of a position to 2 percent of the cash balance of your total day trading account. This 2 percent limit would, in theory, allow you to have 50 consecutive losing trades before your account had a balance of zero (50 trades times 2 percent equals 100 percent).

CHAPTER 13

Preparing for Your First Trade

You can have your skills developed to the point that you have a feel for the market and have the ability to make a plan as to your day trading objectives. Day trading objectives can be set each session, but they should be made for every position with the use of a profit and loss limit for every trade. If you can incorporate some basic risk-management techniques and moving stops, you are going a long way toward being ready for your first trade.

Getting a Feel for the Market

The thought of your first real money trade can be both frightening and exciting. In order to ensure a successful and enjoyable experience, it is best to make sure you are ready. This readiness comes from having a firm grip on where the market is, where the market is going, and how you can ride its movement to capture gains. An honest assessment of your financial market awareness can go a long way in telling yourself if you are ready to place that first trade, and serves as a yardstick to measure your confidence and assurance of the profit of that trade.

Your market awareness should be at the point that you have a few favorite sectors that you monitor on a daily basis. They might be your favorite vacation spot's currency paired with your home country's currency. It might be the price of oil or other commodity that you use on a daily basis. It might be an index of the market itself, either a measure of the S&P 500, the Dow 30, or the NASDAQ.

ESSENTIAL

A really good way to develop a base point of reference for a market's index or individual security is by using your demo account. You could place one trade in your demo account for each of the indexes, sectors, and securities you trade and use the notes section of your trading platform to mark them as baseline market levels.

Because markets and prices are always moving, you can begin to look at the price levels of a sector at any point of your development. This would be your starting point, or your baseline that you made all comparisons in reference to. When in the processes of establishing a baseline for the market, it is best to give yourself time to see a change in the underlying price of the sector. If this is not done, you will fall into the thought that that market is always and has always been at that level.

Watch Changing Price Levels

Much like the fashion world, what seems in vogue during one season, often turns out to be unfashionable and out of style by the next season or fashion cycle. It is best to keep in mind this analogy when evaluating the price levels of a commodity, future, FX pair, index, or ETF. If you watch a sector long enough you will see it change in price, fall out of favor, or otherwise shift in sentiment.

Securities prices are always changing, and when you hold off from establishing a position until you witness this change, you will have a sense of history and knowledge of that sector. It really helps you decide to establish a position in a security when you know that last month, season, or year that same security was 10 percent higher, 10 percent lower, or worse. Long-term observations of the market will firmly root in you a value system of what sectors were worth and how prices can change over time, whether quickly or slowly.

Markets move in patterns as shown in technical analysis, and trading setups can be repeating in pattern. If you do not allow enough time to develop a feel for the market, you will be trading blind, with only your charts and fundamental analysis to guide you. While these are very good guides, a value knowledge of where the target stock, ETF, future, or commodity has been will give you a greater sense of the potential of where they can go, having the potential to both increase and decrease in value.

Making a Plan

After gaining a sense of where the market has been and where it is going, and before you place your first trade, it is best to plan the trade from beginning to end. When you are starting to trade it is often very easy to get caught up in the moving markets and forget your original objective of the trade. If you have a written plan of each trade you will have a record of the entry point, expected length of the trade, expected exit point of the trade, and expected outcome of the trade. Writing down the goals of a trade will give you the most benefits and control of your daily, weekly, and monthly overall day trading profit. Writing down each trade's goals will teach you to enter into each trade with a clearly defined outcome.

You should know before you open a trade at what point you expect to close the trade, and lock in your profits. This thinking through the trade before committing to it will help you gain control over your trading. If this is not done, you will get into the habit of opening and closing trades at any point of the market, with no goal other than to make money. A goal of trading to make money is not a plan. Your day trading should be treated like a business, and the capital in your account should be treated as an asset to reach your goals. In order to reach your goal of having a profitable day, week, or month day trading, each trade should be planned. It is better to have three or four well-planned trades during the day than to engage in a series of rapid-fire opening and closing of trades without any thoughts to their placement.

FACT

Many sports coaches teach their players to visualize personal goals during training sessions. A weightlifting coach might tell the trainees to visualize themselves lifting certain target amounts. A gymnastics coach might tell the team members to visualize making a perfect landing after a vault. Visualization is often a key to many top athletes reaching their goals.

Remember, you are building the balance of your cash account in order to have a surplus in the account, with hopefully enough surplus to make a withdrawal from the account at the end of the month to pay your expenses and give yourself a salary. Successful businesspeople evaluate potential investments carefully and rank each one on its own merit and potential. Even though they might have the means to get financially involved with every deal that comes across their desk, they are wise enough to limit what they get into, and they have learned to be patient to wait for only the best deals. Each trade you enter into is a form of a deal. When a trade is profitable, you can get out of it, and generate additional cash for your account. When a trade turns unfavorable, you are stuck with it. When it closes out at a loss, you are weakening your account and day trading business.

Stop-Loss and Take-Profit Orders

Written plans can be as simple as entry points, expected time in the trade, and exit points. You can take the written plan one step further by setting a stop-loss order and a take-profit order at the time of the opening of the trade. Setting a stop-loss order is when you precalculate the maximum loss you would take in the trade before your trading platform places an automated closing out of the trade, thereby placing a limit on the percentage and dollar amount of the potential loss of the trade.

A take-profit order is the exact opposite: you enter in beforehand the amount of profit in percentage or dollar amount that you would like to make on the trade. When the security meets the price level that is required to meet your preset profit amount, your trading platform will automatically close out the position, and lock in your gains. Both stop-loss and take-profit orders are keys to planning a trade, and are very good tools to use in effective active risk management of your day trading account.

Setting Your Profit and Loss Limits

The proper planning of a trading day always includes a review of the markets while scanning for potential day trading setups. After taking note of the setups that are available, you should then move on to choosing the best of these, and then go about the business of planning each trade before placing the orders. When you are ready to commit to a trade, call up the place order screen on your trading platform.

The order screen will have fields for the symbol of the security, number of units, and the price at which it will execute. In addition to these fields there are fields labeled "Take Profit" and "Stop Loss." As you enter in the number of units of the trade, the trade value in dollars will show as well as the margin used. Before the submit button is pressed and the trade is executed, you can lock in your planned profit and limit the potential loss involved in this trade.

Using the "Take Profit" field, you would enter in the price of the security you would like to have the trading platform close the order automatically, which would lock in your gains. As you can see by the view of the trading platform and order entry screen of the FX trading site ONADA, the order is for a long position of 17,500 units of AUD/JPY in the FX market. The current price of the trade is 77.477 (meaning that one unit of AUD, the base currency, is worth 77.477 units of JPY, the quote currency. FX is always priced by taking the first currency, in this case AUD, and dividing it by the price of the second currency, in this case JPY), giving the trade a value of $14,794.32 using $295.89 worth of margin at 50:1. The take profit has been entered in for a quick turnaround and is set at 77.745. The order-entry screen shows that at this Take Profit price this trade will yield $56.93 in gains when the close order is automatically triggered.

You wouldn't take a trip to a foreign country without telling someone where you were going and when you would be back. You can tell yourself where you are going with a trade and when you are coming back by setting profit and loss limits ahead of the trade.

The next step you would take would be to use the stop-loss field of the order-entry screen to set the maximum amount of loss that could occur with this trade before the trade was automatically closed out. Although stop losses automatically close out trades at a loss, this loss amount can be programmed to be small in relation to your overall account dollar size.

Risk Management and Moving Stops

With a proper risk-management technique such as the **2 percent rule** and pyramiding, the planned use of stop losses can prevent and control a major meltdown in a trade position. The 2 percent rule is where each trade is preprogrammed through stop losses to close the order with no more than 2 percent of your total account balance lost.

For example, you have a $10,000 balance in your account, and you have an order on the books for 100 shares of an energy ETF at $10 per share for a total of $1,000. You would place a stop loss order at $8 ($10,000 x 2 percent = $200 maximum loss. $1,000 total position – $200 maximum loss = $800 mimimum ending trade value. $800/100 shares = $8 per share). It takes a bit of working out on a calculator, but this method can be a very effective risk-management tool.

This is a good example of a setting your expected profits before the trade is made and a good example of day trading with a plan. You would make this trade after consulting all relevant market indicators, news, and charts to get to the point where you were reasonably certain of a favorable outcome of the trade. Of course, there is the saying of "Cut your losses and let your profits run." This refers to the technique and strategy of moving your stop losses up as the price of the security moves up.

For example, if you place a trade for a stock at $15 and a stop-loss order at $12.50, you are $2.50 behind the market price of the stock. As the stock moves up in price, you would move the stop to exactly $2.50 behind the moving market price of the stock, i.e., if the stock moved to $18.75, you would move your stop to $16.25. This would trigger a closing-sell order at the new price of $16.25, and would lock in $1.25 in gains. As the stock moved higher from $18.75, the stop loss would be moved higher yet. This is referred to as a moving stop and can be a very effective tool in keeping your profits intact in moving markets.

Risk-management methods such as the 2 percent rule and moving stops are a key element to keeping you in the game of day trading. Too many times day traders have built positions without regard to risk and have lost considerable amounts of money when trades went bad.

There is often an option on your order-entry system on your trading platform to make a moving stop activate automatically: you can set the percentage, PIP, or dollar amount that you would like to use. Your trading platform then automatically creeps the moving stop up as the security moves up (or down, if you are shorting or selling the security). The combined effect of watching the market, looking for setups, reading the charts, planning each trade, and the active use of stops can lead to very profitable day trading, all while limiting your risk.

Know When You Are Ready

Finally, you will ask yourself, "Am I ready to make my first trade?" You will never be able to answer this question fully without the acceptance of some risk. Not every day trading opportunity is the perfect chance to make money. Day trading is not an absolute science. If you have been studying the fundamentals, watching the markets, and reading the charts, then you are ready to trade. Starting with small dollar and margin amounts will take the pressure off of your first series of trades and will allow you to get into the markets sooner rather than later.

CHECKLIST FOR YOUR FIRST TRADE:

- ❏ Read your broker's overall market reports
- ❏ Check the daily market news
- ❏ Monitor the long and medium timeframe charts
- ❏ Watch the trends
- ❏ Plan your entry and exit points
- ❏ Place the trade

It is important to have your first day trading experiences work out to be positive ones. Starting small and getting out of the trades early with even the smallest amount of profit will enable you to have the experience of enjoying day trading on your terms. You to do not have to start out with big, do-or-die type trades in order to have the feeling of being successful in your day trading career.

Don't jump into a live account. Much money can be lost in the first few days of day trading if you are not 100 percent fully ready for the action, excitement, and pressure that it takes for day trade with a live account. Keep your money safe for as long as possible by practicing day trading in your demo account first.

Remember, you are using a building approach to develop positive experiences day trading, all the while giving yourself the chance to make profitable trades as you go along. The worst thing that could happen is if you tried too hard and placed too many big trades all of a sudden, and these trades resulted in rapid losses from your account. If you aren't patient and somewhat relaxed in your manner during your first few trades, then you will be setting up a habit of approaching your day trading sessions as a time of tension, frustration, or worse yet, panic.

Some Goals of Day Trading

You will know when you are ready to make your first trade when you can approach day trading as a business that you find very enjoyable, exciting, and profitable. Of these three, day trading should be enjoyable, first and foremost. When you identify the goal of day trading as enjoyable in your mind you will be moving away from constantly looking for the profit rush, a feeling of euphoria that comes about when a profit is made in the markets. This profit euphoria can be quite addicting, and can lead a day trader to take on greater and greater risks or position sizes in search of greater and greater gains.

Even hardened traders will have a bad day. They handle it by knowing they are armed with their best judgment, but sometimes the market goes against them. When this happens, they go back and evaluate the risk level of every position they are in. Keep this in mind when you get the urge to increase the risk in your account.

This mentality can be destructive to your profit and loss statement. There is only so much profit that you can squeeze out of an account of only so big a size. In order to pass this natural profit amount per day or week from the dollar amount size of your account, it is necessary to take bigger risks through larger margins, concentrated positions, etc. This is not good business and not a way to turn your day trading into a career. You should learn to start small, manage risks, limit margin, and know your profit and loss points all with the thought of learning to day trade. With careers, there is no "one big trade." That is stuff of Hollywood and fantasy. In order to make a living at day trading you must make small, measured profits day in and day out.

With the effect of making more winning trades than losing trades at the end of the period, your account will show an overall profit. This should be your second goal. The last goal should be excitement. You will learn that this excitement comes naturally whenever you are dealing with money and the markets. It can be thrilling to day trade. Mastering a sector, knowing a product, following it in the news, and then making money by day trading the product you know so much about can be very fun and satisfying. This should be considered a measure of how well you are taking to your new business of day trading.

If at any time you do not feel the same excitement making regular, risk-managed, relatively safe trades, and you feel the need to thrill seek by changing margin ratios, taking bigger bites of a position than you are used to, or getting into exotic products, *beware*. When this happens, you are taking your successes and profits for granted; this attitude can be very destructive to your account. If this happens to you, take a few weeks off. Withdraw some of the money in your account and buy something fun, or take the family on a vacation. In this way you will get some use out of the money you would probably lose if you started to take increased risks before you were ready.

CHAPTER 14

Building Positions and Risk Management

Position building and risk-management techniques go hand in hand. You can take steps to limit and control the amount of risk you are taking with each trade and each position. A very popular method of building a position while limiting risk is the use of the pyramid method. After you are in the trade, effective uses of stop losses and take profit stops will help you quantify and limit the amount of loss possible on a trade, all the while locking in the profit target of the position.

Buying the Cheaper End of the Trade

A good thing to remember when you are thinking about entering into a trade is the fact that you are buying the cheaper end of the trade. What this means is that the product that you are in, whether cash, a stock, ETF, or future is more expensive than the product you are buying. For example, if you are in cash, and you are thinking of buying a stock, then the cash is priced higher relative to the price of the stock. If you have a stock that you are thinking of selling, then cash is priced lower than the stock. In other words, when selling stock, cash is a better value than the stock. It is the cheaper end of the trade.

In order to find out which end of the trade is the cheaper one, you need to know quite a bit about security analysis, including fundamental analysis and technical analysis. Often, though, when trading a security for a long time, you will develop a gut feeling of what is the cheaper end of the trade.

This system is a really good way to value any purchase or sale of a security. Ask yourself, what's the better value, the cash or the stock (ETF, etc.)? Even thinking of entering into a currency pair, you should ask yourself, which currency is the better value? (Or, what's cheap? What's expensive?) By answering this question, you will prevent getting into a position that is at the top of its value against what you are selling. Buying the cheaper end of the trade is a good system to help you decide if a trade is worth getting into, and deciding when to reverse the trade and go back into cash.

Risk Management

The use of risk management can be a very effective tool to keep your account intact, even after a series of bad trades. The system that is best used is one of limiting position size, limiting concentrated positions within industry sectors, and using stops effectively. The goal of effective risk management is to develop a system of using a bit of math to get your positions built and closed in a profitable way while minimizing the chance of losing money. While the market can turn against you, and trades can go bad, you can follow some steps to limit losses.

The first method is to limit position size. This is true if you are using an equity broker, an FX broker, or a futures broker with or without margins. Think of your total amount of available trading value to be no more than 20 percent in one position. If you have an account with a $50,000 value, and you use one-half margin, you will have a buying power of $75,000. If it is your normal procedure to use 50 percent of your buying power at any one time, the total amount you can have for one position is $75,000 x 50 percent = $37,500 x 20 percent = $7,500.

Risk management is often one of the most misunderstood departments in an investment bank. In a big investment bank there are all sorts of traders who are building positions in their own sectors. The risk management function of the bank sometimes acts as the police, preventing any excessive buildup of a position across the company.

This 20 percent rule is a good method to force you to diversify your positions to no less than five positions at any one time. This diversification between securities will go a long way in keeping your account intact. Twenty percent is the high end of the position size rule, and a drop in the percentage to 15 percent or even 10 percent will further enhance the diversification of your day trading portfolio. In addition to limiting position size and therefore diversifying the securities you are trading in, you should limit concentrated positions by diversifying across industry sectors, or even products. This can be achieved by bundling all of your positions in each industry, such as energy, metals, financials, retail, etc., as one position. This is done because there is a good chance that all of the securities within an industry will go up or down at the same time according to the market's movements.

If you are in three positions in the banking sector, then you would further enhance your risk management by bundling these together as one position. A second level of risk measurement would be to bundle the markets in which the securities trade, such as equities, commodities, or FX. Remember, you are trying to get a snapshot of your overall risk and trying to quantify the overall **uncorrelated diversification** of your entire day trading portfolio. The uncorrelated diversification of your day trading portfolio is when you have different positions spread across many securities, industries, and markets, so that when one trade turns bad, it is supported by many others that are not related or affected by that trading/market event or news.

Using Stops Effectively

Another method of risk management is the proper use of stops. A stop is an automated sell order that is programmed into your trading platform at the time of the trade's placement. An account's risk can be measured in the percentage that the stops are placed behind the entry price. For example, if you enter into the ETF QQQQ (the Nasdaq 100 Trust) at $50 and you place the stop for that trade at $45, the stop will automatically sell QQQQ when it gets to $45, limiting your loss on the trade to $5, or 10 percent.

Won't the placement of stop losses make me lose money?
Stop losses do the exact opposite. While it may look as though you are selling out of your position at a loss and losing money, their real purpose is to prevent you from losing even greater amounts of money if the position moved a large percentage against you.

If you place all of your stops at 10 percent below the entry price of your trades, you are, in effect, limiting the loss of your trades to 10 percent across the board. If you are using 100 percent of your tradable assets, and you only have ten positions, you will zero out your account after ten losing trades in a row. For example, you have a $1 million account with ten trades each of $100,000 in value. If you place the stops at 10 percent behind the entry price, your trading platform will automatically sell out the positions with a $10,000 loss. If all ten trades went bad and were automatically closed out, the total loss would be $100,000 x 10 percent = $10,000 x 10 trades = $100,000 loss in total. As you can see, this $100,000 loss is 10 percent of the total fund. You are limiting your total losses to 10 percent of each trade with this system. If you continued along with these position sizes (100 percent of the account with ten trades total), you would have to lose over 100 trades in a row to zero out your account (this does not include the trading costs).

The use of stop losses is a form of defensive risk management. An offensive-orientated risk-management technique is to program your trading platform to automatically sell your positions at a predetermined profit point. This will lock in your gain and help you to plan ahead how much you would like to make from each trade. For example, you could program your trading platform to automatically sell a security at a price that is 10 percent above the entry point. This price can be programmed in as a percentage or dollar amount before the trade is actually placed. The fields in the order entry window of your trading platform would be filled out as to dollar amount or percentage of gain, and you would then place the trade, and wait for the automated sale at the profit point.

Run the Business Like a Casino

Here is some food for thought: if you believe that the markets are completely random, are volatile, and are affected by many, many factors, you could make it your trading philosophy to run your day trading business like a casino. Casinos make money by providing gambling where the house plays the odds. If a game table has a 2:3 odds, the gambler will win twice for every time the house wins three times. If you think of yourself as the "house" and if you believe that the markets are totally random and a game of chance (which some do), you could set all of your trade stops to any odds you would like. If you wanted 2:3 odds, you would set your stops to a ratio of 2:3 with the higher being the take-profit order.

For example, you could buy QQQQ at $50, set your stop loss at 4 percent behind the entry price and your take profit at 6 percent above the entry price (2:3 ratio). If the market was totally random, you would make an automatic 2 percent on every trade (lose 4 percent gain 6 percent equals 2 percent net gain.) In order to get this system of randomness to work properly you would have to enter many trades to get the averages to smooth out and the statistics to be spread evenly. A study can be made with a sample set of as little as 100 trades, but the higher the better. This might be a good experiment to set up in a dedicated practice/demo account.

Using the Pyramid System

The pyramid system is a method of splitting your building of trades into three different time periods, thereby in theory giving yourself three different price levels. It is similar to the dollar cost averaging theory of investing, but each of the three trades is on the books separately, instead of grouped together.

Deciding on Trades

To use the pyramid system effectively, you would first identify a potential trade. Second, you would go through your risk-management calculation to determine the total position size that would be appropriate for your account. You would then divide this dollar amount into three trades spread out during the course of the holding period. If you are buying an ETF and you determine that the trade setup will last two days, a one-third entry point would be made at your initial signal point. If you are trading DIA (the Diamonds-Dow 30 trust) and you determine a buy signal at 110, you would buy in one-third of the total calculated trade amount at this price.

Don't eagerly jump into a setup with one big trade. With setups there is often a tug of war going on with the day traders across the globe, and the effect is to push the security up and down until it starts to move in one clear direction. Until that happens, stagger your entry points with the pyramid method.

As the price of DIA moved with the up and down movement of the Dow 30, you would make another one-third buy in at a price that appeared favorable. Since the Dow 30 may be moving upward during the trading period, the second and third buy in doesn't have to be at a lower price. The system is not intended for you to buy in at three lower prices, rather it is intended to spread out your entry points if the security falls in value allowing you to have additional capital to invest at the lower price. Three different priced entry points will give you an extra cushion of risk management that can be very helpful in limiting your exposure to a falling market. Positions that are broken up into thirds are also easier to enter psychologically, as it is easier to emotionally commit to a trade if you know that you have a cash reserve to buy in at lower prices if you misjudged the opportunity for the trade and the market moves against you.

Closing Out Trades

The pyramid system can be also be used to close out trades as well. Your total position would be divided into three equal parts. As the total position turned profitable you would begin to close it out in three trades. This dividing up the closing out into thirds would lock in your profits but at the same time allow for the further growth in the gains of the trade. As the trade gained further, the second one-third would be sold off, locking in at that profit point, leaving the last third to be closed out at the next point. The combined effect of buying in thirds and selling in thirds can be a very effective risk-management tool, as it spreads the cost of the trade over time and prices, acting as a smoothing agent to the overall cost basis of the position. At the same time, when it comes time to close out that position, the pyramid method will allow you to lock in your profits while giving flexibility to capture further gains in a moving market.

How Many Positions at One Time?

When you are just starting out, you may find it very helpful to only have between one and three positions open at one time. This is due to the fact that when you are first starting to day trade you are learning to identify and interpret all of the market indicators that go into making successful and profitable trades. For example, you will be monitoring the short and long-term charts and the market news while at the same time remembering the overall big picture information, such as overall market trends as well as security and economic fundamentals.

Keeping the number of trades you have to the minimum will give you enough time to react to all of the market's developments and how they relate to your trades. At first you might find that watching the market develop and seeing it make your positions (and fortunes) go up and down a bit thrilling and overwhelming at the same time. It takes some time to realize that it is real money in your account, just as it takes time to learn how to feel the emotions of winning and losing trades.

It often takes time to be able to comprehend all of the information on a trading screen. If you are starting out and you have too many positions open at one time, you might suffer from fatigue very quickly and have to end the trading session before the exit point of your trades.

If you keep the number of trades you have open to three or less, you will also be allowing yourself time to analyze each trade after it has been closed out. Your goal at first should be to have enough trades and positions open to give yourself the training to have multiple information inputs and situations to follow, but at the same time not to have too many things going on as to lose track of good trades, or worse yet, suffer from information overload.

Moving to More Positions

After you have got the knack of day trading with three positions, you can gradually move to higher amounts of total positions open. Keep in mind, however, that when you have a great deal of trades open and you are using margin, you are running the risk of the losses compounding into your margin account even faster. For example, let's say you usually trade five currency pairs, commodities (a gold ETF) and equities (an S&P ETF.) You have your currency account set to a margin of 50:1, and you are using the following risk-management parameters: at 50:1 margin, total FX positions will not exceed 33 percent of available margin at the time of the trade. You trade the gold ETF and the S&P ETF in an equity day trading account with 50 percent margin max. You decide to use the additional use of across sector risk management of one-third commodities, one-third equity, and one-third FX in your total investment portfolio.

With this ratio you are able to have $4,995 in commodities (gold ETF), $4,995 in equities (S&P ETF), and $11,088.90 in each of the currency pairs or crosses per $10,000 in your total day trading account.

Gold ETF	33.3% x 1.5 margin x $10,000 total day trading account	= $4,995
S&P ETF	33.3% x 1.5 margin x $10,000	= $4,995
FX Pair	33.3% x 50:1 margin x 33.33% total FX margin available	= $11,088.90

FACT

The compounding of positions on themselves was one of the factors that lead to one of the most famous hedge fund collapses of all time. The Connecticut-based hedge fund Long Term Capital Management was using this compounding effect in their hedge fund; when one of the positions fell suddenly, it caused the rapid unraveling of their entire portfolio.

More Risk-Management Techniques

Further risk-management techniques would be dividing the market long, short, and neutral position into further thirds. One-third would go into a bucket of market long positions: long S&P ETF positions, long AUD/JPY, AUD/USD, and USD/SEK positions, etc. One-third would go into market short positions: long gold ETFs, short AUD/JPY, short USD/SEK, etc. The last third would be in market neutral positions, such as the soft commodities and grains, and the FX pairs with a market neutral bias (EUR/SEK, EUR/CHF, EUR/NOK, AUD/NZD, and USD/SGD). Additional risk management could be the additional purchase of an alternative investment mutual fund that uses a market neutral global macro style, such as UBS's Dynamic Alpha (BNACX). Dynamic Alpha is a mutual fund that is managed as a hedge fund, and has extensive use of derivative overlays to neutralize risk and give a market neutral bias. Consider the addition of an alternative investment fund as a buffer in your overall day trading account, acting to further smooth out peak highs and lows due to concentrated positions. A position in a market neutral alternative hedge fund–styled mutual fund would be held for the medium-longer term, and consist of around 10 percent of your total portfolio.

Profits, Losses, and Your Buying Power

The total buying power in your accounts will be constantly changing, moving up and down as the value of the trades in your account moves with the market. With higher leveraged trades such as futures, commodities, or FX, your total buying power will be affected greatly by the number of open positions in your account and how well they are doing. For example, when you first buy or sell a position to open, you are committing cash and margin to the trade. When the trade becomes profitable, more margin will be added to your account in proportion to the amount that the trade is in the profit zone. The gain in a trade actually allows you to buy or sell more positions to the open with the additional margin created with the gains. To review, margin is used to buy a position to the open; as it moves into a profitable position, the gains are added to your account (unrealized gains). This additional account value is then interpreted as additional margin available, and therefore additional buying power.

Using a High Rate of Margin

If you are using a high rate of margin in an FX or futures account, the gains will equate to even more amplification with the use of margin on the available buying power. Example: you have $10,000 in an FX account. One of your trades used $2,000 in margin, and at 50:1 the position has a total value of $100,000. As the trade becomes profitable, the gains are added to your account as more margin. If you made 2 percent on the trade, the gains would be $2,000, and this would be added to your account. This fresh $2,000 can be then spent on an additional trade at 50:1 or another FX trade with a value of $100,000. The process would be repeated with each trade's gain until you had huge positions built upon higher and higher leverage.

The problem with this trading philosophy and style is that the risk is amplified higher and higher and eventually comes to the point that your whole account would have multiple positions all built on the gains of the trade before them. If the profits in percentages and dollar amounts were impressive with the multiple leverage method described, the losses in the account would be equally as impressive and equally as dramatic if the market turned against you. As the prices of the FX trades came down, the positions would unwind very rapidly and your account would collapse the weight of its own leverage. This is essentially what happens to some major hedge funds and other major financial institutions when there is a shortcoming in the risk-management departments. It is a form of maximum profit generation, and when done right for short times (often through automation) it can lead to very high returns, but it can also lead to an account's rapid destruction.

CHAPTER 15

Developing Your Own System

Thinking of day trading as a business will help you develop your own system of studying the market before committing capital to a trade. If you are using a method of looking for setups in order to increase your returns, preventing trading fatigue by switching markets, and learning from each trade, you are practicing a system of day trading that the experts use. Knowing when to walk away from day trading is also an element of a good day trading system.

Treat Trading Like a Business

It is best to think of your day trading activity as a business. This means that your business (day trading) should be self-sustaining. After the initial setup costs, learning curves, and other necessary time required to learn the business, your account should pay for itself. To simplify this thought, you should take your ending account balance and subtract your beginning account balance. This will give you your net gains for the period or month. You should then subtract all of the expenses directly related to the generation of those profits. These are your expenses. You should, on average, have a net positive number. This number might not be very large at first, but as long as it is a positive number, you are making money with day trading.

If you are in a period where you are recording losses in your account, don't despair. Some of the world's largest and most profitable investment banks report quarterly trading losses. This is especially true during strong market turbulence and difficult trading environments. If this is the case, it might be a good time to walk away from the markets.

This profit is not the only measure of a business. A measured approach to risk taking, the gradual addition of more capital, and a cool headed, businesslike approach to winning and losing in the markets are other hallmarks of treating your day trading career like a business. It can be helpful to read books on the subject of running a home-based business to help you get into the mindset of having a business, profit generation, and limiting expenses. Some things to consider are keeping business hours, having a dedicated office area, keeping good books and records of all expenses related to the business, and possibly working out ways to day trade while raising a family.

Running a Home-Based Business

Even though you are working in an industry that is worldwide, deals in large sums of money, and uses mass amounts of information and high technology, you are, essentially, running a home-based business. If you were running a home-based painting contracting business, you would evaluate each and every possibility to bid on a painting job with your ability to finish it with a profit in mind. You would figure your costs, length of time for travel to and from the job, and risk level to come to a total price of the bid. If the customer did not take the bid, you would walk away from the job as unprofitable.

While there is emotion involved when your capital is at stake, it will help if you think of yourself as a professional trader and be somewhat detached from trading. You are trading for profit, not for entertainment; when you are a professional trader you are paid on your profits, not on the number of trades you enter into haphazardly in hopes of something working. There are times a professional trader will sit, with a mug of coffee or tea, and watch the markets all day without entering one trade if he knows there is no money to be made that day. Preservation of your capital should be your number one goal when you run your day trading like a business. This means you do not trade for fun, you do not put your account at too great a risk, and you avoid trading in securities that are not showing clear indicators.

Study the Market, Then Trade the Market

It should be a goal of yours to have a system to help you get ready for a day trading session. This system can act like a checklist to go through before committing your first dollar of capital that day. The first item on the checklist should always be to study the market. This "study first, trade later" idea is one that is prevalent in some form whenever there is a certain expertise level required in a bourse type of environment. Whether you are a rare coin dealer, a jewelry merchant, or a dealer in vintage motorcycles, if you know your product and your market well enough, you will be able to spot many buying and selling opportunities and go far with your trading business.

The same is true for day traders. The idea is to become so versed in your field that you can check the price of a future, ETF, currency pair, or stock at any time, from anywhere, and know if it is a buying or selling opportunity. Without this level of knowing your market you might sometimes find yourself in a situation of missing a potential money making trade due to your inability to reference it to its value.

Studying the market is to become an expert in it; think of it like a subject to master before taking the test of making trades with real money. This mastery takes a lot of study and time at first, but like the big investment banks, you will quickly be able to exploit your market knowledge in both offensive and defensive ways, both protecting your capital and adding to your capital through profitable trades.

Mastering Your Subject

After your initial study of the terms of the market and day trading, move to studying the economy in general and the sectors specifically. When you feel as though you have a good enough understanding of how the market works, you are ready to trade. Start small at first, and try to make every trade a learning experience from spotting setups, to buy in, to close. Day trading is a subject to master, and a day trader treats his job as a career and profession.

If you are going to be away from day trading for a few days or even weeks, keep track of the market news by reading *www.marketwatch.com* on your smart phone. If you don't keep tuned into the market, information can pass you by, as the market can change very quickly.

If you were to do the same, you would invest in your education and the time it takes to get trained. This training takes time and money and might equate to studying setups and the market as often and as regularly as possible, and with it, the commitment of capital and its exposure to actual trades. If you were to go to a top university as an MBA to study the markets in hopes of getting a job as a trader in one of the big investment banks it would take you anywhere from one to two years full time and $50,000 to $100,000 in tuition expenses. Many people consider this as a good investment in time and capital, as there is a potential to make a great deal of money as a trader.

Consider what others are spending in time and money on the pursuit of their careers. It is good to have a reasonable expectation as to how long and how many trades it will take before you are running at full steam, and making one good trade after another.

Looking for Setups for Higher Returns

One of the greatest sayings in trading is "make money by sitting on your hands." This adage refers to the fact that often, money is lost by reckless trading by buying or selling of securities in an account. Even though you may not have a full-service broker and the structure of your account may be with very low commissions, you can buy and sell too often in your own account without thinking the trades through, or worse yet, out of boredom or a desire to gain excitement through day trading. Entering into the markets to trade without looking for setups is the quickest way to end your day trading career.

Search for Setups

You must learn to "look before you leap," and search for setups. There are two things that are essential to a profitable day trading session: good setups and free capital to commit to the trades. If your money and margin are tied up in a grouping of positions that weren't thought out, but that were entered into haphazardly, you are running the risk of tying up that capital and margin, possibly in losing positions. Your goal is to preserve your capital first, and to have winning trades and to make money second; not to trade for excitement, or for an experiment.

If you are going about day trading in the right way, you would have available cash and margin always waiting on the sidelines, always available to enter into a good setup when one becomes available. Always look for the best play of the day before you enter into a trade.

Recognizing Days Off

Sometimes this means the market is flat, sideways, or otherwise not giving any good indicators as to good setups. On these days it is best to continue to be "at work" but not day trade. Use those days to review your past trades, with the casual following of the markets in the background. Sometimes, if there are no setups at the early part of the markets opening, then seasoned day traders will take the rest of the day off. Their logic is that money that is not lost in bad trades or otherwise used on a flat or bad market day will be there for the next trading session. In fact, it is often said it is all right to not trade during these kinds of market sessions, to not feel as though you are required to trade each day, and that the markets will be there when you come back.

There are some classic stories of traders who are not in the market for weeks on end, all the while checking into the charts and news looking for setups, with their cash sitting on the sidelines, earning interest, and not engaged in any trading. These traders trade less frequently, as they are looking for bigger gains with larger amounts of committed capital. This cruising for setups is a mindset that will go a long way in keeping your account's profit and loss statement positive longer. There are fewer times to make really good trades, and more times in which capital can be tied up in flat markets, or worse yet, unprofitable trades. Trading is a lot like fishing with more than one pole. You bait your poles, put them in the pole holders, and sit at the shore, waiting for a bite. As long as you are searching for setups, you are profitable. Only enter into trades that have good setups brewing, and ones that are leading to a profitable situation quickly.

At first, sitting on the sidelines will seem unproductive, but with time and experience you will see that many of the lower-end, lower-yielding trades go nowhere, never develop into a profit, or end up being losses. It could be a good training aid to trade in your practice demo account when you encounter lower end trades in a sideways market. This will help satisfy your desire to trade and at the same time give you a chance to learn with a "what-if" scenario.

Switching Markets to Get Refreshed

You will find it helpful to switch the markets that you scan for trades once every two or three months. This will allow your mind to view new patterns and to study new trends, which can be very refreshing. Most people have a tendency to rotate among the same two or three securities looking for setups. You might have your favorite currency pair, ETF, or commodity.

After the initial balancing act of going among your favorite sectors looking for profits is reached, you could suffer from a typical trader's problem: boredom. You could find yourself looking for the next best thing once your mind and emotions get used to the level of excitement that comes from day trading your usual securities. It is common for people who get to this point in their trading careers to seek out the feelings of when trading was new: this is often done by increasing the risk of the day trading account by increasing leverage. These feelings of wanting to increase risk can best be handled by switching among sectors or within sectors to trade. This will once again give you the feelings of excitement. Moving into a new sector such as day trading commodity futures after trading commodity ETFs is an example, as well as exploring currency pairs with different fundamentals that you are familiar with, such as away from the major pairs and into the European crosses (EUR/SEK, EUR/CHF, and EUR/NOK).

How do I know if I am a thrill seeker, or just enjoy day trading?
Thrill seekers enjoy taking risk. They will seek out the good feeling they get by taking risks and will often put themselves and others at risk because of their need for thrills. Enjoying trading, on the other hand, means you take calculated risks and have a respect for the markets.

There are other ways to keep fresh, such as looking at different sources of day trading information, subscribing to new newsletters, or even switching the periodicals that you read. Another method of staying fresh with your day trading perspective is to simply take a month off. It is often the feeling of being comfortable that allows you to become complacent with your risk management. If you go on a vacation with some of the money you have built up in your account, you will come away with a feeling of having splurged; this alone is often enough to make you take less risk and work harder to make successful, high yielding trades. Believe it or not, enjoying the money that you have built up in your day trading account is just as important as building up the account in the first place!

Learning from Each Trade

You should keep a record with entries for each and every trade and the market conditions that are associated with it. It can be a simple notebook with a separate page for each trading session, or it can be one of the commercially available preprinted forms for the purpose. Here are some things to keep track of:

- U.S. indexes
- Overnight Asian and European indexes
- Weather in New York, NY, and Chicago, IL (if you are trading commodities)
- Gold price in USD
- Price of EUR/USD
- Price of USD/JPY

After writing down the overall market conditions of the trading session, you would begin to list each trade on a separate line. You would list the buy in price, the exit price and the expected gains. This trade-record system will help you analyze the trades you have made after they have been closed out and will give you a base to measure them against over time.

ESSENTIAL

Using your past trading information to gain further knowledge is a form of testing your theories. It is actually a form of back testing, which is a method of setting parameters and testing those theories with past market data. This testing method is often available with your trading software, allowing you to electronically back test day trading ideas.

Reviews of your transactions should be made at the close of each trade or at the close of each trading session at the minimum. Learn to compare the good and the bad equally, as there is a lot to learn from profitable as well as unprofitable trades. Some of the things you are looking for are if you spotted a setup correctly, if you placed your entry price and exit price correctly, and if the time it took to make a round trip in the trade was what you thought. You are also trying to spot trends in the overall market conditions versus your positions, so try to notice patterns with this element. At first when you are trading, things will seem random, and it will be difficult to determine if a trade will become profitable once you enter it. You will find it easy to see how your predictions of the market's directions have played out and how the overall market conditions affect your positions. Writing down your trades also keeps your day trading in a businesslike mindset, especially if you treat your record as a trade blotter of an investment bank that could be shown to a potential investor, or to an imaginary manager who would be trained to look for an effective use of the bank's capital.

With appropriate records, you have more to show for your work at day trading than just a positive number in the profit and loss section of your trading platform: you have a diary of the daily workings of your day trading company, with all of the profitable and losing trades, and market conditions that allowed you to spot the setups in the first place. Lastly, good records will go a long way at the end of the year when you are filing your taxes, as these types of records are an absolute requirement when it comes to building a profit and loss statement.

When to Walk Away from the Markets

Learning how to walk away from the markets after a good trading day is a key element in keeping your perspective fresh and piqued with interest. If you have had a particularly good run in the market you should get into the habit of closing out all of your positions, summing up all of your trades, and allowing yourself to feel good about what you have accomplished by day trading. When good fortune comes your way from your own thoughts, planning, execution of trades, and reading the markets, you should be very proud of yourself: You are on your way to mastering the art and science of day trading.

You might ask, what's the best time to walk away from day trading? The answer is simple: whenever you get a thrilling feeling, you are in a state of elation and shocked as to the amount of money you have made from trading. This is the best time to take a break and put your winnings in a safe place, such as the money market or 100 percent cash. When you close out all of your trades and put the proceeds in cash, you are giving yourself a cooling off period. This time is best spent going to the beach, shopping, or taking the kids to the zoo. Your goal is to do anything other than look at your returns, your cash balance, the charts, or the market's news.

Let the idea of winning big in the markets sink into your mind while relaxing without the distraction of any further trades. Even the British Army's Special Forces, also known as the Special Air Service (SAS), are taken off patrol for a mandatory twenty-four-hour cooling-off period after a successful engagement. The SAS has learned that the troopers are jumpy and pumped with adrenaline after having the opportunity to successfully accomplish what they have been trained so hard to be good at. In this way, you can think of yourself as a commando: much training goes into getting ready for the actual target event, the successful capture of gains through day trading.

ALERT

When you are walking away from a bad trading day or series of bad trades, try not to keep too much negative emotion with you. The more negative you are when you leave the trading desk, the more difficult it will be to return at a later date.

The Cool-Down Period

When a big mission is accomplished you too need a cool-down period. Without this cooling-off period, you would look at the markets for the next setup with eyes filled with emotion. After a big win or series of big wins the market will look different for a while, i.e., you might see an "impossible market" where you wonder how you could ever make money again, or you might go in the opposite direction and take added risks to get further excitement from day trading. If you have either one of these viewpoints, you must keep in mind that the market has not changed from before, only your perspective has changed. Take time to feel good about your day trading successes. The experience of having the ability to be in 100 percent cash, take a calculated risk, make a profit, and reduce the risk to zero by returning to 100 percent cash can be very empowering. This empowerment takes a few days to sink in completely and is part of the training process of learning how to make a living at being a successful day trader and living the day trading lifestyle.

CHAPTER 16

Advanced Trading

Learning and using advanced trading techniques can amplify the returns in your day trading account. Once you understand the relationship of the time length of a trade and overall returns, you can begin to build short timeframe, overnight trades, carry trades, and scalping into your day trading methods. Applying concepts of advanced trading further will allow you to use your trading platform to program automated entry points. These methods are easy to learn and can add up to more profitable trading sessions.

Time Length and Overall Returns

It is good to keep in mind the returns of investing in the stock market over the years and the returns that can be generated by putting your money in an FDIC-insured CD when thinking of the returns available with day trading. Granted, you are not investing by definition, and you certainly are not saving, but it is good to compare the yearly returns of the three. With the FDIC-insured CD your money will be safe, but the returns will creep along with a slow compounding rate.

CDs usually compound once a month, meaning that the interest is added to the principal; the interest payment is recalculated after that, and so on. CDs pay anywhere from less than a 0.1 percent to 5 percent a year depending on the interest rates of the economy. On the other hand, the historical average for keeping your money in the S&P 500 for a year is around 10 percent annually. With both of these calculations, the time length involved is a year. When you are day trading, the returns can be anywhere from 0.1 percent to over 10 percent, but the length of time that it actually takes to make the trade is often less than a day. Many times, the length of holding the security to generate the returns can be a few hours.

FACT

The Dow 30 went down 34 percent in 2008, and this was its worst performing year since the Great Depression back in the early 1930s. This was due to the banking crisis of 2008–2009, a crisis that almost turned Wall Street and Main Street into a panic. If only you would have shorted the market with a 2x or 3x bear ETF!

If you are holding a security for a day and you are making 1 percent on the trade, you would annualize the returns to make a comparable against the returns for the CD and S&P 500 investment. The calculation would be the return multiplied by the holding period in days multiplied by 365. If your trade was held for one day and returned 1 percent, the annualized return on the trade would be 365 percent. If you held the security for 6 hours (one-quarter of a day), the annualized returns would be 1 percent x 4 x 365 days = 1460 percent. If you were in a carry trade that lasted one month (one-twelfth of a year) and your returns were 20 percent, your annualized returns would be 20 percent x 12 = 240 percent.

As you can see, the length of time that you actually hold the security determines the annualized returns. These annualized returns are the reference required to make an accurate return-per-trade comparison to CDs and the "buy and hold" returns that are quoted by the media. Keep in mind, though, that by no means should day trading be considered an investment: there is a considerably higher degree of risk associated with day trading and the use of leverage, but the goal is to quantify the returns on an annualized basis. Once you have the annualized returns, you are able to better compare the percentage returns your day trading is making.

In addition to the returns, once a trade is closed out, and the funds are ready to trade with again, you will have a higher balance in which to trade with and to use margin with. This has the effect of compounding your money, but the compounding is done very quickly (within the day or a few days) as opposed to compounding once every month, quarter, or year. The combined effect of the high returns matched with the frequent compounding can lead to very dramatic gains over a month's or year's time.

Short Time Length "Squat" Trades

The shorter the time length that you are actually in the trade, the lower the expected percentage movement of the security is. When you get to very short-term trades of a few minutes, securities do not have that much time to move in any direction dramatically. To compensate for the small percentage movements that happen in ultra-short timeframes, commit larger amounts of margin and dollars to the trades.

These ultra-short timeframe trades can be thought of like when a weight lifter squats a barbell over his head. The weight lifted in a squat is very heavy, and is hoisted over the athlete's head in a short, quick, clean, jerking movement. Also, the goal of the squat is to lift the heavy weight only once: squatting is not an endurance sport. If you have this perspective in mind, you would load on more than the usual amount of margin and money (the heavy weight) with the intention of getting out of the trade after a slight upward movement in the security. If the amount you have in the trade is large enough, you could close out the trade very quickly and still make a good profit.

It is true that this type of trading leads to a situation of having concentrated positions in your account by having large amounts of your capital tied up in one or two trades. This indeed goes against the usually recommended risk-management techniques of using smaller amounts of capital per trade and diversification of positions across securities, sectors, and market bias. You can use a modified form of risk management when using the high dollar/margin trades. This risk management would include only having one or two trades open at the same time, and the use of very tight stops.

How much of my total margin/cash should I use on short-term trades?

Your combined margin/cash amount for all of your ultra-short-term trades should be no more than one-third your total amounts of margin/cash available. If you have $10,000 in your account, have no more than $3,300 committed to anywhere from one to three positions in this type of trading.

The use of tight stops means that you've programmed your trading platform to close out the trade when the price of the security is very close to the buy-in price. Both the take profit and the stop-loss orders would be programmed in before the trade was made, and you would predetermine the gains on the trade in dollar amount (after transaction costs) beforehand. The dollar amounts of the gains can be very small as compared to the capital involved in the trade: what you are looking for is small, quick gains made in a timeframe of five to ten minutes or less.

Markets have a way of just creeping along very slowly when you are trading in these short time periods. It is important that you do not take your eyes off of the profit indicator of your trading platform when you are doing this kind of trading. In fact, it is recommended that you call up the close-order screen as soon as the order is opened with thoughts of closing out the trade soon thereafter.

The longer the trade stays open, the more risk that other traders will force the security to move against your position. It is best to think of getting into a trade that is moving, and getting out very quickly. If the trade does not move, or the market is taking a breather, your best bet is to get out of the trade. Remember, the shorter timeframe of this type of trade will give you an added risk-management function. Your motto should be to get in and get out very quickly. If the trade doesn't perform in a few minutes, exit out of it: when you do this the only thing you will lose is the transaction cost of the trade. This is a small price to pay for being risk averse with your account.

Overnight Trades

Normally with day trading, your account starts with 100 percent cash at the beginning of the trading session and is back in 100 percent cash by the end of the trading session by closing out all of the positions. There is a different type of trading that involves the overnight markets, usually in futures and FX accounts. In order to trade overnight, look at the developments in the markets that are open on the other side of the world. If you live in the United States, markets are usually traded in the early morning till the early afternoon.

You can get some good news and indicators as to what the developments will be in the Asian and European markets from late in the night. To trade overnight effectively, program your buy and sell orders into your trading platform in the evening. The program executes the trades automatically for you when the trade enters into buy or sell points while you spend the night sleeping.

Some traders make it a habit to get up early in the morning before the U.S. markets open to see if any of their orders have been filled. If you follow this method, you can find your trades placed, with sometimes both the opening and the closing taking place, and wake up to a profit in your account.

The other variation on this method is to look at the developments of the world's stock markets for the previous few sessions and decide if the world's markets will be up, down, or sideways for the next session. You would then buy into the future or FX pair that follows the markets' risk sentiment, and place a sell order near the buy-in price. You would determine the direction of the markets by the indicators of the Asian markets, which open around 7–8 P.M. Eastern.

If the world's markets have been in an upward movement for a few days, and there has been a big run up in trader's risk sentiment, then the currency pairs that follow this risk sentiment will have also been up during this time. If you check the Asian markets after a few days of the U.S. and European markets being up, and the Nikkei, the Hang Seng, and others are down, there is a good chance that the world's traders are selling off some of their positions and taking their profits. You might decide to short the risky currency pairs and go long on the risk averse pairs and commodities such as gold.

ESSENTIAL

You might find placing trades for overnight fulfillment to be very stimulating. In fact, many day traders find themselves getting up in the middle of the night to check if their order has been filled. Better yet, some traders put their trading platforms on "audible," which allows their trading platforms to announce "Order Filled" when an entry point is made.

Your Trading Strategy

An appropriate overnight trading strategy in this situation would be to short AUD/JPY, EUR/SEK, and USD/SEK. These currency pairs follow the markets very closely. When the stock markets are up, they will be up; when the world's stock markets are down (when the market is said to be risk averse), they will be down. A good hedge in this scenario would be to go long on a gold future or short an S&P 500 future.

The goal is to place your trades before the traders in Europe and the United States wake up, analyze the markets, and begin to sell off, causing a lessening in risk sentiment of the markets. If you make currency trades, enter your stop loss-stops close, and take-profit stops with a medium distance from the buy-in price, as FX can move as much as 0.5 percent to 1.0 percent overnight.

This seems like a small amount when compared to equities, but remember, you are using high amounts of leverage in your FX accounts: a 0.5 percentgain at 50:1 leverage will yield a gain of 25 percent on your investment. This means you will return 25 percent on the dollar for every dollar of your actual money in the trade. Overnight trading can be a very profitable way to trade the equity index futures or FX, as the indicators can be easy to read through the activity of the Asian markets, before the European and U.S. markets are even open.

Long Time Length Trades

Longer time length trades are trades that last anywhere from three days to a month. With this type of trading your goal is to build up a position over time with several accumulation points. These accumulation points would be buying more of the security at trigger points throughout the holding period. You might have in place a simple buy-on-the-dips trading philosophy.

This buying on the dips is actually a very hands-on technique that keeps you in the game of watching your position develop. The goal is not to have an accumulation of a huge position with no regard as to what you will eventually sell it for. Rather, you would have a selling point in mind, and a value at which, when the security falls below this point, you would accumulate more, much like in the pyramid method. The difference would be that you would divide your buys into three to five prices, but when you sold out you would still sell out with three equal sales amounts.

If you are in the process of setting up a long time length trade, do not let the trade just sit on the books if it falls below a certain loss amount. Just as with any other type of trade, you should still be setting stop-loss orders to prevent a long time length position from becoming a big loser.

This longer-term timeframe trading method is good for seasonal security setups and FX carry trades. Some good targets for this longer timeframe would be gold futures, gold ETFs, as well as the energy securities, all of which are good movers during the late fall and into the winter. You could accumulate the energies on particularly warm days, when the prices of heating oil and natural gas tend to move downward. This accumulation would be done with a target selling date as well as a target selling price.

Potential Trades

If you were buying energies, the target selling price might be in mid-December, just as the temperatures started to fall in the eastern United States. If you were accumulating gold, your selling target might be at the end of the year or even late January, as the price of gold historically moves up at the beginning of the winter and continues until the spring.

An example of an FX carry trade might be to go long AUD/JPY, AUD/USD, NZD/USD, etc., or any combination of a buying a higher yielding currency by selling a lower yielding currency. Trades such as this allow you to accumulate the interest differential on a daily basis as well as the upward movement in price between the currencies. The interest differential in trade can add up quickly and can act as a form of downside protection in an FX trade.

This works because with FX carry trades you are borrowing in a low-yielding currency and parking the amount you have borrowed into a high-yielding currency. For example, you could borrow the USD, and pay an interest rate on the borrowed amount. The interest rate on borrowed USD might be 1 percent annually. You would then move this money in AUD, a historically higher-yielding currency, and earn anywhere from 3.5 percent to 7 percent annually, depending upon the prevailing rates in Australia at the time. The rate you are earning in the carry trade is the difference between the two: AUD minus USD. If you earned 5.5 percent on the AUD and paid 1 percent on the USD, you would earn 4.5 percent annually on your trade, just in interest. Remember, you are leveraging your money from anywhere from 10:1 to 500:1 in an FX account. If your leverage was 100:1, the yield on the trade would be 450 percent on the actual equity involved (the amount of actual cash put up for the trade). Not only would you enjoy the carry trade returns, interest rate is usually calculated and rolled over on a daily basis with FX accounts, even on weekends.

Scalping while Watching the Evening Movie

Scalping is a trading technique of moving small amounts of money into and out of trades very quickly, with the average trade lasting ten minutes or less. It is best done with three to five positions open at any time with the thoughts of gently gaining little by little throughout the trading period. It can be a casual way to spend the evening, as you can trade FX on your laptop while watching the evening movie. With even the smallest account balances, scalping can be fun and profitable. Commit only 5 percent or less of your total buying power to each trade; with five of six positions open, you should not exceed 33 percent of your total buying power at any one time.

Some brokerage firms have strict guidelines as to your trading. These guidelines are set to regulate the effect of very large dollar amounts of scalping. If you plan on doing any amount of this type of trading, check first with a broker you might be deciding to open an account with, as they might regulate scalping.

You can switch from each chart showing the different securities you are watching, but make sure you are looking at very short timeframe charts, one five minutes or less, for a trend overview, and then switching to fifteen or thirty seconds after you are in the trade. You have to learn how to get the technique down to do it effectively.

How to Place the Trade

The best bet is to open up the place-order box and move it off to the side of your screen to make room for the charts. Watch the fifteen- or thirty-second chart to show that trading has slowed and that the market is taking a breather. Next, get the trade ready to go, including number of units, leverage ratio, and long or short. Put you cursor over the place trade button.

What you are waiting for is the security to move suddenly away from the point at which it was resting: You want to place the trade at the beginning of the movement and close out of it at the end of the movement. These will be your setups, and although most setups use fundamentals as well as technicals, there is none of these in this type of trading. You are just looking to capture the short-term movements, regardless of the overall fundamental or technical indicators. In and out within minutes with small amounts of money: It is a safe, fun, and quick way of earning extra returns for your account, and over the course of the time it takes to watch a few movies, you could add up some real earnings.

Programming Your Trades for Automated Entry Points

After you have mastered the art of looking for setups, and manually entering into trades, the next thing to master is programming entry points into your trading software. This is done to automate the trading process and to allow you to be a bit more hands free on your trade entry during a trading session. You would still look for setups as normal by listening to the news, reading the journals, analyzing the fundamentals, and looking at the technical indicators.

Once you have determined that a security is good to trade and has the potential to be profitable, you then move on to determine a good entry point. Before this, you were making market orders; in other words, you were entering in the trades at whatever point the market was at the time.

When you are programming your trading platform with automated entry points, you can set the length of time in which you would like the order to stand. For example, you can have the order be good for the week, where as if by the end of the week the order is not filled, the order is automatically canceled.

When you program your trading platform to make limit orders to open, what you are doing is only committing to the trade when the security makes that price or better. You can analyze the price of the security ahead of time and determine the best price to enter to make the highest return. If an ETF is at $48, and you determine that you would like to buy 300 shares at $46.25 or better, you would enter into a buy limit order at this price. The trading software would tell your broker that the order was outstanding and in place. When the ETF reached this price, your order would be executed automatically, even if you were not at your day trading desk that session.

You could couple the automatic order entry with the automatic closing out function of your trading platform. For example, you could enter in a buy order at $46.25 and a sell order at $48.25; this order would be activated once the stock or security was purchased and would remain active unless the order was closed out manually or canceled. While it is best to remain as hands on as possible with your analysis, looking for setups, and day trading, it is possible to automate the process. Remember, you never want to automate the buy- and sell-order decisions in your account. While you can automate the actual entering and exiting of the trades, it should be your own thoughts as to when and what to buy or sell in your account. There are plenty of companies that promise great returns by offering the use of their proprietary signal service that tells you what and when to day trade. Your goal is to own your account, and to own your day trading profits and losses. It is only when you are making the decisions for your account that you will be able to make a living, day trade as a profession, and own your profits.

CHAPTER 17

Evaluating Your Performance

You might be curious as to how you are doing after day trading for a while. Day trading has a learning curve, and it takes time to master building up and closing positions in an active market; this is especially difficult when dealing with real money. To measure how you are doing, you will first have to learn how to calculate returns. After this, you have to realistically look at your performance, and determine if trading is enhancing your income.

Remember, That's Money You're Talking About!

It is good to keep in mind that your account is funded with real money, and that your profits and losses are composed of the same money that could be used for buying things or for paying bills. With this in mind, you should view your profits in terms of what it is worth outside of the world of day trading and outside your account. For example, if your account has a balance of $20,000, you are trading part time in the evenings, and your profits for the month are $500, that is a return of 2.5 percent. Perspectives shift, and depending on how you look at it the $500 return can be both good and bad.

Don't get caught up in thinking your account balance is too small. The amount of money that would be considered a lot when spent on other goods often seems to be very little when spent on day trading securities. Perhaps this is a function of looking at numbers on a computer, rather than holding money in your hands.

With the bad perspective, you have only gained $500 in your account against a balance of $20,000. You might think that the money and time you have spent learning the markets, looking for setups, and watching your trades develop should yield an amount that is greater than the $500 you see in your profit and loss. In fact, with this perspective, if you invested as much time in your day trading job per week as you would in an average part-time job (20 hours a week), you would actually be making about $6 an hour, which is less than minimum wage. If you have this negative perspective, you would give up on day trading all together. Certainly, if you were in it for a competitive hourly wage, you would begin to think you were in the wrong business.

Think Positive

On the other hand, if you looked at your $500 return in a positive light, you would realize that you returned 2.5 percent of your capital in one month, and if the situation continued and the returns stayed the same, your account would have a balance of almost $27,000 at the end of the year, and a compounded return of 34.5 percent annually. Considering that the average return for a buy and hold strategy including the S&P 500 stocks would average a return of around 10 percent per year, the 34.5 percent returns you would have made day trading part time are good.

Also, while it is difficult to day trade with the constant monitoring of the markets, keeping up on the news, and looking for setups, most day traders would tell you that having a job of day trading is much better than a job in which you have to show up for work, punch a time clock, and collect a salary. Day trading is a lifestyle, and if you have a first few months or quarters of making $500 in your account while trading part time, you are off to a good start. More gains will come with time and experience. It is often not necessary to add funds to an account to achieve higher returns: rather it can be a factor of getting used to a new sector, being familiar with market indicators, and even the season in which you are trading. With the proper perspective, you can think that any amount of your gains means that you are learning, doing well, and navigating the world of day trading for a living.

The Mathematics of Calculating Returns

When calculating returns you have to look at the core dollar amount that is in your profit and loss for the days, weeks, and months, with the overall thoughts of looking at your returns on a monthly or quarterly average. The reason you look at your returns on a daily basis is that in annualized percentage terms, you might have stellar performance in your day trading account.

If, for example, you are in a trade that returns 2 percent of the dollar amount and the percentage amount, it might seem small at first glance. When you annualize the returns, the numbers can change dramatically, and this is due to the ultra short holding time of trades when day trading (usually a few days or less).

If you are to calculate the annual returns on the 2 percent gain you would take the 2 percent daily return and multiply by the number of days in the year, 365 = 730 percent annualized returns.

To be even more technical, you would take the return in percentage, divide it by the number of hours holding time of the trade (assume three hours), multiply this number by twenty-four hours in a day, and multiply this number by the number of days in a year (365).

2 percent divided by three hours = 0.667 percent multiplied by twenty-four hours = 16 percent multiplied by 365 days = 5840% annualized returns when calculated on an hourly holding period. Although this is a not a standard method of calculating returns, it is a way of equal comparison, as the returns on a bank CD or savings account is calculated on the stated return with the compounding periods calculated, whether it be daily, monthly, or quarterly. In banking and finance terms, this number is called the nominal APR or annual percentage rate.

FACT

Banks and other institutions use many different methods of calculating returns. Most are done to calculate the annual return. When you are comparing your returns to that of other investment vehicles, make sure you are using the same method as quoted by the institution. This will ensure a comparison of "apples to apples" and not "apples to oranges."

This nominal APR is the number that is calculated by the straight percentage times the number of periods in a year. Although a bank CD or a savings account is not in the same risk category as day trading, it is good to use the same mathematical method of comparing yearly returns between the two. Comparisons of APRs will allow you to more realistically judge your performance in a way that can help you determine the return of each trade.

Your Total Monthly Performance

On the other hand, your total monthly performance is a truer indication as to your overall performance, as there can be good days and bad, and over time they will average out to more accurate performance measure. To calculate this number, take your account value at the last day of the month, and subtract the value that it was at the beginning of the month. This is your gross profit or loss for the month. From this number, subtract your expenses to arrive at a net profit or loss. This net profit/loss should be divided by the amount that was in the account at the very first day to arrive at a percentage gain for the month. The same is done for the yearly profit and loss calculations.

Of course, there could be two scenarios. The first is that your dollar amount of profit is high, you are covering your bills, and you're earning enough to draw a salary from the gains. The second scenario is that the dollar amount is small, you are covering your bills associated with day trading, but you are not making enough to draw a salary. If this is the case, focus on the percentage returns. If they are high, but the dollar amount of the return is low, consider the fact that you are doing well and are mastering day trading; it just might be that your account balance or amount of total margin cannot produce higher dollar returns for the amount deposited. If you are in this situation, be patient—you are doing well; it is only a matter of time before your account grows to the point of being able to throw off enough self-generated cash for you to be able to take a salary draw.

Realistically Looking at Your Performance

In order to realistically measure your performance in day trading you will need to look at the percentage of your monthly returns as well as the actual dollar amount of your gains. In addition to these quantitative measures there are the psychological benefits to day trading and placing winning trades in the market. You should look at the combination of these to get a feel for how you are doing in the market.

How do I really know how I am doing with day trading?
Only you can answer how you are really doing. You can't really compare your returns to that of any other investment, because day trading is not a buy and hold strategy. You may find the benchmark Dow Jones Credit Suisse Hedge Fund Index helpful: *www.hedgeindex.com.*

Keep in mind that it is very difficult to make consistent profits day trading at first. It might even take you a half a year or longer to learn how to consistently make a profit day trading. In this introductory period, it is really important to positively reinforce your skills, and this can be done by having the attitude of "looking at the glass half full." It is impossible to give yourself a goal as to the percentage or dollar amount you will make in any given period, whether a trading session, month, or quarter.

Get into the attitude of searching out any positive way to look at your day trading experience while you are learning how to trade. If this means being happy with a $100 gain in one trading session, or a 10 percent gain in your account in one week, or even ten winning trades in a row, it is up to you to stay positive. Use the good feelings to keep yourself motivated and enthused about your new day trading career. For example, you should look at every positive experience as very good no matter how small. This is a really good habit to get into, and will go a long way in keeping you motivated and learning about the markets and making fresh, well thought-out trades.

Breaking Even Is Okay

If you are looking to break into day trading as a profitable part-time job or as an exciting career, the first thing you will need to do is get your day trading to pay for itself. In other words, if it costs you the price of a computer, news subscriptions, and a separate Internet line to run your business, then you should be able to make enough profit in your account to cover these expenses. If the actual book cash outflows (not the same as expenses) equal $30 a month in periodicals and newspapers, $75 a month in high speed Internet, and $45 in computer fees and extras, you realistically need to clear $150 a month in gross profit a month by day trading just to break even.

Notice that the business use of your home, the business use percentage of your utilities, or your salary is included in this number. This is because the dollar amount you should use is the actual cash outflows of the business (and your household) generated by the operation of your day trading business. It would be even better to multiply your monthly expenses by three and use this number as your base line for each quarter of operation.

If your actual cash outflows are $100 per month, you need to clear $300 in gross profit calculated every quarter in order to make sure your business is breaking even. Keep this goal in mind when you are going from day trading session to day trading session. You might, in fact, make this goal in the first few days or week of the quarter; everything after this is profit.

ESSENTIAL

If you are breaking even in your account, don't despair. During these times, look at your day trading business as a hobby. There are very few hobbies that are directly associated with the news and allow you to have an active part in your financial future; also very few hobbies have the potential for as much profit as day trading.

Allow a Breaking-In Period

Remember, you have to allow yourself enough time to get trained and learn how to day trade the markets. There is a lot to know, a lot to think about, and a lot of technical expertise required to day trade profitably. With this in mind, you might be worried if you are getting ahead, learning enough, or making enough money.

If you are going to allow yourself a breaking-in period, having a bare minimum target number will help you reach your goals quicker. You could take your financial control one step further, and withdraw your base expenses from your account as soon as the number is reached. For example, if you need to make $525 each quarter to cover the minimum of expenses, you would continue to day trade each session until your account balance was up $525 from your account balance on the first day of the quarter. As soon as this dollar amount of profit was reached, you would stop trading for the day; you reached your breakeven for the quarter. You could put in a withdrawal-funds order to transfer the $525 out of your day trading account and into your checking account. After you've done this, take the rest of the day off. You've done well; the rest of the quarter is pure profit. This is actually a good form of risk management, e.g., don't day trade with your bill-payment money.

Is It Enhancing Your Income?

A good way to determine if you are getting anything out of day trading is to see if it is adding to your income on a monthly basis. This is the ultimate goal: to be successful enough at day trading that your trading generates enough cash to make a withdrawal above and beyond your basic expenses. Your day trading activities could be set up in any number of ways that are good for you.

For example, you might day trade futures from 7 A.M. to 3 P.M. every day with a $75,000 account and be on your way to your first six-figure salary, or you might trade Forex in the evenings with a 100:1, $1,000 account, content to make enough profit to pay for this month's car payment and a dinner out. Anything above the breakeven point is profit, and should be considered a very good thing.

The professional day traders at some of the big investment banks earn around $100,000 per year in salary. Where they really make the money is at year-end when the companies they work for hand out performance bonuses. Some of these bonuses can be anywhere from $500,000 to $1 million per year depending on how the trader did for his bank.

To analyze it further, and to truly determine if it is enhancing your income, you would have to recalculate the net profit of your account with the added burden of a comparable salary. If you are trading part time, or better yet, while enjoying your favorite show on TV, then you would calculate zero as your comparable salary, since you are not missing any wages by day trading while watching an evening movie. On the other hand, if you have given up a job to day trade full time, it is appropriate to add in your lost wages associated with the time spent day trading, not going to a full-time job, and not collecting a salary.

Determining Day Trading Value

There are of course lifestyle benefits to working at home, day trading in the markets, and owning your own business. Only you can quantify the dollar amount associated with the many benefits you are receiving by day trading. While it is difficult to put a number on the actual dollar amount you are foregoing by day trading full time, it is important to try to put a value on yourself. Calculate this dollar figure into the additional amount of money that you need to make to determine if you are ultimately enhancing your income by day trading.

It might be that the difference between what you are making in the markets after expenses is comparable to going to work for someone and collecting a salary. If you are at this point, and can get there by taking an appropriate risk/reward ratio, then you would be in a very enviable position by your peers. Most people would like to be able to make money with their assets, and most people would like to be self-employed. When you get to the point with day trading that you can consistently earn profits with appropriate risk, your business pays for itself, and you have the choice of drawing a salary or compounding your profits all while working for yourself, you have mastered the centuries old craft of using capital in a productive and profitable way.

The Day Trading Learning Curve

Learning about the economy, the markets, and how to day trade takes time. You can expect to spend several weeks or even months to get to the point where you feel comfortable to make your first small trade, but your real market knowledge will not set in until you are actively day trading with actual money for several months. You might even find that after six months you are still learning the subtleties of day trading and all of the subjects that go with it, such as pyramiding, money management, and risk management.

It is good to start your day trading off with a smaller amount of money and learn to day trade profitably before making additional deposits to your account, allowing you to trade with large account balances. This is due to the fact that it will take you time to learn to read the markets, spot setups, and technically enter and exit positions properly. It is good to give yourself time to learn the basics, as market conditions and setups usually develop slowly.

ALERT

There is much information available out there for you to study and read to help you get trained for day trading. Just because someone or some company offers a complex system of trading that is difficult to learn does not mean you will have guaranteed results. The best systems are often the simplest and easiest to learn.

For instance, spot the opportunity for a longer carry trade developing. Even though the carry trade might be a very good trade to make, you would still have to wait to make the appropriate entry point, usually after a consolidation in the market, or a point of selling off where traders are taking their profits, causing the price of the currency pair to fall. On the other hand, you might be patiently watching the S&P 500 futures gain in price for weeks on end as they follow the overall good feelings in the market. You might spot this as an opportunity to short S&P futures, in hopes of capturing value when the market stutters, stalls, and corrects, falling a measurable percentage.

Take Your Time

It is also good to keep a realistic budget of time to allow yourself to get trained to take on more complicated trades, or move from simpler day trading into trading that involves more complex issues. A good example of this would be giving yourself three months of trading equities and ETFs before moving into leveraged ETFs with 2:1 or even 3:1 gearing. After getting a good feel of how a leveraged ETF reacts to the markets, you could include the day trading of some of the bear ETFs that are available. After learning how to use equities and ETFs to learn the basics of order entry, leverage, and shorting the market, you can move on to day trading Forex, which would increase your available leverage ratio (from 10:1 to 500:1) and easily give you the ability to short currency pairs. On the other hand, if after learning to read the market reports and analyze the fundamentals and technicals, you might want to move on to day trading some of the smaller-sized lots of futures available, such as the E-mini S&P 500, and the E-mini commodity futures.

The overall goal is to give yourself enough time to have experiences winning and losing in the markets with a manageable amount of leverage, and enough capital to feel the full emotions of day trading. Do this before moving into higher leverage, higher dollar amount accounts and riskier, faster moving sectors. You should look at day trading as a long-term goal. With this in mind, take every precaution to ensure that you will be there to trade the next day with your account and wits intact.

CHAPTER 18

Emotions and Trading

After you have been day trading for a while you will most certainly feel the full emotions of winning and losing money in the markets. If you learn how to master these emotions, you can take advantage of other trader's feelings about the market. You should, however, know that you shouldn't day trade when the market upsets you, as this will cloud your judgment. Lastly, you should know the truth of the risk versus reward myth, and how to know and manage your risk limits.

The Emotions of Winning and Losing

Money made in the market is a very special thing. It can give you a feeling of empowerment, a feeling of being wide awake, and a feeling of control. It is a form of alchemy in a way, where you are using your mental energy, intelligence, and the electric power of your computer to make money multiply. Most of your trades will be well thought out and planned, and occasionally some of them will yield very high returns. These high yielding returns are the positions that have a magical quality—you planned them, but they worked out better than you imagined. Once one of these trades has gone a full turn (trade opening, gain, closing, and realization of the profit) there is no going back: you will most likely be bitten by the day trading bug and the seemingly effortless way in which money is made.

The Thrill of Success

It is an amazing feeling to make a capital gain in the market. In fact it often feels as though the gains you make in the market are making something from nothing, which when you stop to think about it, can make you have feelings of power, euphoria, or even a feeling of being a master of the markets. This is why some traders at the big investment banks are often referred to as "Masters of the Universe."

Money that is made from day trading is technically not a capital gain. For income tax purposes, money made from trading is categorized as ordinary income. This is because when a security has a round trip (the opening, holding, and closing of a position) of less than one year it is considered short term, and therefore considered income.

When you feel these feelings for the first time, remember that there is a certain element of your trades that are based upon your planning, knowledge, and intelligence, and there is a certain part of each trade that is based upon unpredictable market factors. If you keep the unpredictable-market-factors part of the equation in mind, you will be well on your way to having a successful day trading *business, and not be trading for emotional gains.*

Granted, there are a lot of good emotions that come from day trading and making money; these should be the components that keep you trading, they should not cloud your judgment with inflated egos and the pursuit of higher and higher risk levels. This is precisely why it is recommended that you walk away from your trading terminal after a big session day trading in the markets.

Just as the emotions can be really high after making a big winning trade, your emotions can be equally as low after a big loss, or a series of bad trades that draws your account down. If you have been following some risk-management procedures such as using stops, pyramiding, and limiting position size, you should be able to walk away from a series of bad trades with more bad feelings than actual lost money. To go further with this thought, if you have been day trading with money that has been set aside for this purpose, and not have been using money that needs to be used for necessities such as rent, etc., then your low emotional state should outweigh your lost economic status. Emotions are the name of the game with trading. Your goal is to think as coolly and as businesslike as possible with day trading while at the same time allowing yourself to feel the highs and lows of winning and losing in the market.

Do the Opposite of What You Feel

One of the key parts of trading like a professional is learning how to think logically when emotions are running high. In some situations it can be said that you know what needs to be done with a trade, but your feelings are telling you opposite. If you can flat out coldly separate your emotions from what you have learned and have been trained to do, you can enter into very unruly markets and gain from them. This is a form of advanced trading when you are trading in unsettled and very volatile markets.

For example, in the spring of 2009 the S&P fell several percentages for a few days during a time of extreme market duress and bad banking crisis news. Most traders and investors were pulling money out of almost all sectors at the same time, which left a very precarious situation of rapidly falling worldwide markets. If you were a day trader at this time, you might have been very emotionally motivated to keep your account safely parked in cash (and even then you would be worried about the safety of your balance!). If you were thinking logically and were willing to take a small measured risk, you could have had a small amount of your account placed in a highly leveraged long S&P future.

Be careful: Trading in volatile markets sometimes leads to what is called a wash sale. A wash sale is the sale of a security at a loss thirty days before or after the purchase of the same security. Any losses from a wash sale are disallowed according to IRS regulations.

In this instance, the S&P turned around dramatically and gained over 10 percent in one session, which would have realized you a heavy gain, all by doing the opposite of what you felt the market was reacting. This is an extreme case from the recent past, but many professional traders will tell you that the market often sends out very negative signals just before the best setups happen and profits are to be made.

Trust Your Training

Often, doing the opposite of what you feel means doing what you have been trained for and what is logically right. If you know that markets are overall reactionary and emotional in nature, you can learn to exploit the negative emotions that run commonly in the world of trading. Two of the most common negative emotions are feelings of fear and greed. Fear is the emotion that you will lose your money in bad market conditions, and greed is that you will lose out on a perceived gain by remaining in the markets past the normal growth of a position. Learning to use logic and go against the normal feelings you have can guide your day trading to becoming very professional in nature. It should be a goal to be as logical and as opportunistic as possible with the appropriate risk-management procedures in place. Some of the large investment banks and hedge funds throughout the world are using this method to the extreme—they attempt to use computer programming and automation to predict outcomes and execute orders using statistics, higher mathematics, and mathematical logic. While these are extreme cases, you can take a cue from some of these methods. To apply pure logic to an emotional animal such as the world's markets and do so with a cool conviction can be a very difficult task. If mastered, the effects on your profit-and-loss tally sheet can be impressive.

Don't Trade When the Market Upsets You

If you find that the market is upsetting you in any way, whether from losses in your account, bad market news, or difficulties with your interpretation of economic data, by all means, shut down your trading software and walk away from your day trading area. It is normal to experience times when things seem overwhelmingly negative, and this can give you a feeling that it is very difficult to progress toward your goal. When it comes to a time that things are not going your way and you are unsure of your next action with your day trading account, no amount of mental concentration or emotional might can make things go better. What you need to do in these times is refer to your backup plan. Since your day trading business is your business, and you are your own boss, you do not have to feel as though you have to squeeze each and every possible trade out of bad trading days.

Trading during volatile times can lead to stress. It is good to use exercise to help you get through emotionally upsetting markets. Going to the gym, playing outdoor sports, mall walking, and even cleaning out the garage can help you relieve stress, as the physical activity can help you refocus yourself toward positive thinking.

This is exactly why there is a saying in the professional day trading world of "sell in May and go away." Since the professionals know there are times when there are no setups on the horizon, they have backup plans, ways to enjoy life and not try to grunt their way in the market searching for returns that aren't there. The world's markets have begun to get more and more volatile since the late 1990s. This can create times when there is a lot of money to be made with relatively safe trades; it can also create times when a lot of money can be lost on even the most tame, well thought out positions. When the market is bad, and it upsets you, don't feel forced to trade harder to make up for lost opportunities. Setups should come easily, almost gently, and should not be forced or upsetting to make. Your day trading business should work for you, and add to your lifestyle, and is not intended to cause you undue strain or grief.

In that frame of mind, keep an overall barometer of your feelings toward the markets and day trading in general. If you feel yourself getting worried, overwhelmed, or otherwise upset, do yourself and your account a favor: allow time for yourself to feel good again about trading. No one needs to take unnecessary risks, and if you are day trading under duress you will not be thinking through your setups and trades properly. Remember, day trading should add to your lifestyle, it should make you feel good about yourself and give you a feeling of empowerment from your profitable handling of money. If there is a period of time that this is not what you are getting out of your business, then give yourself permission to take some time away to get a new perspective.

Use the Market's Emotion to Your Advantage

Most times the market is operating in a well-organized manner with predictable unidirectional sector moves. Other times, the market can be quite emotional and can be behaving erratically. These times of extreme upward and downward movements can be an excellent opportunity to keep a cool head and make money getting into trades at the bottom or top of valleys and peaks. These emotions come in two forms: euphoria and panic. In the euphoric stage, most all market participants are sharing the same good feelings: the market is going to go up, up, up! Euphoria in the markets can come and go very quickly. All it takes is one bad piece of information to end the good feelings of traders and they will take their profits, or worse yet, begin shorting their positions. Your goal should be to spot these euphoric feelings and short the sector they are in, or even short the whole market with a bear ETF, shorting an ETF, or even shorting an S&P 500 future.

On the other hand, panic can also take over the mood of the markets causing very steep declines in short periods of time. These are usually brought on by sudden reports of bad news, sometimes global news, due to a natural disaster, or political problems. During these times the market can feel very upset, and the bad mood might flow out into the mood of the general public as well. These times can also be a good time to begin building long positions in the affected market.

If you are going to build positions either to the long or to the short of the market or sectors during these times, it is good to keep in mind that while there is a very good chance that the market will change direction, it is often impossible to determine when the change will actually take place.

QUESTION

How do I safely build a position in a panicked market?
You would build your positions using the pyramid method, but instead of three entry points, you would use around four to six spread out evenly over the length of the market's panicked mood. You would, however, use the standard three-point exit strategy to close out the position.

To counteract this time of uncertainty, take smaller than usual bites of the sector and use the pyramid method, but with your accumulation spread out over longer timeframes, such as a week to ten days. The goal is to set up a longer timeframe trade much like an FX carry trade that takes up to a month to go from start to finish. If you are building a position on the extreme dips (long positions) or peaks (short positions), the total return of the positions can be impressive when the market corrects itself. The key is to build the trade so as to not be detrimental to your account if the trade goes against you for a while; stops can be used, and total margin can be limited to prevent extreme downward swings in value.

How can you tell it is a good time to build a position in the market during these times of highs and lows? You will know when the news of the market flows into the daily conversation of the general public. The market and its sectors are usually only discussed by the general public when they are at extremes. When all is rosy and it seems that there is "free money" to be made trading in the stocks, FX, and commodities, everyone will be talking. Conversations will be started in line at the grocers, at the bookstore, at the dentist's office. When things are going really good, Main Street gets involved, for better or for worse. If the market is really bad, these same people will talk about how the market will never come back, etc. The key phrase to listen for is, "things are different now." This is a sure sign that the market is either at a peak or a valley, people are feeling either very good or very bad, and that it is a good time to go in the opposite direction in the market. Much like doing the opposite of what you feel, if you do the opposite of what the market feels, you can have impressive returns in your account.

Risk versus Rewards

It is often said that you must assume risk to get a reward. This statement is only partially true. It leaves out the fact that there is a limit to the amount of return that can be gained from a unit of risk, and that often, with diversification, risk can be reduced while enhancing returns. This concept of limiting risk and enhancing reward was first introduced by Harry Markowitz and his paper **Modern Portfolio Theory**. In 1952, Markowitz mathematically proved that risk could be reduced by the movement away from single securities and toward the inclusion of non-correlated securities into the portfolio.

FACT

Modern Portfolio Theory is based on many assumptions: one of these is that the correlations among assets will be fixed and constant forever. This part of MPT was challenged during the banking crisis of 2008–2009 when most of the world's markets and asset classes' betas became correlated with each other, causing many traders and investors to hold undiversified portfolios.

The inclusion of non-correlated securities in his model portfolio had the effect of reducing volatility while keeping returns at an optimum level. Securities were measured as to the unit of correlation to the overall market (S&P 500) by the Greek letter ß (beta), where as when the security moved 100 percent in tandem with the market the ß would be 1.0, if it moved half as much the ß would be 0.5 and if it moved twice as much the ß would be 2.0, etc.

Modern Portfolio Theory proved that if you included securities that had different levels of ß, the returns of your portfolio could remain high, but the total risk (measured in aggregate ß) could actually be below the risk of if you invested in one security at a ß of 1.0. This is significant as it proves that it is not necessary to take on added risk to get the most efficient portfolio.

To translate this theory to day trading, think of your overall account value, i.e., all of your accounts with all brokerages as one big portfolio. In your overall portfolio, you can make the addition of lower beta securities and still obtain a high level of potential return in your accounts. Your positions might include an S&P 500 position, commodities, market sensitive FX positions, and market neutral FX positions. Using different layers of risk "buckets" measured in ß, you could build an overall portfolio that would include high risk, high return, high ß positions; medium risk, medium ß positions; and lower risk, lower ß positions. Using a bit of math, you could calculate your overall account's beta to arrive at a number. The goal is to have a desired potential return while having a ß of 1.0 or less. This ß of 1.0 or less would mean that your risk was at the same level as trading an S&P 500 position (often referred to as "the overall market").

The difficulty comes in coming up with a realistic measure of any one of your positions in terms of beta. The beta of equities and ETFs are found easily on finance websites; others can take a bit of research and work, but betas can be estimated via proxy. For example, you can derive the ß of a currency pair in an FX or futures trade by looking up the ß of some of the currency ETFs that are available to trade. After a bit of practice, educated estimates can also be made for the other sectors. Some sophisticated trading subscription services offer the ß of most every tradable asset and sector available.

Know Your Risk Limits

When you are setting up a portfolio of positions or placing an individual trade, it is important to know your individual risk tolerance. If you are starting to learn how to day trade, you might want to "de-tune" your strategies and only enter into trades that are of a lower risk nature. When you are just starting out it is important to have adequate time to develop positions and not to have too many fast moving, volatile, and risky trades open. This will give you more mental room to think about how each trade is reacting to the market's news and other developments.

De-tuning your accounts and limiting the risk in your day trading sessions can be as easy as using less of your overall portfolio's cash balance, day trading three uncorrelated asset classes, or even limiting your trading times to sessions when only long positions will be profitable.

Keeping your trades simple and being more risk averse will make each of your day trading sessions move slower, with the overall effect of bringing more comfort and enjoyment to your day trading business.

Day trading with real money in fast moving markets is stressful and filled with pressure. If you can learn to ease these factors by limiting your risk, you are going a long way in keeping your day trading sessions positive experiences, and ones in which you can learn from and build on.

Don't feel as though you have to be trading with high levels of margin, with unfamiliar sectors, or high dollar amounts. If you feel comfortable starting with minimal risk at the price of smaller returns, then this system is good for you. Once you get the gist of analyzing market news, studying the fundamentals, reading the charts, and day trading successfully, it is easy to search for higher returns by increasing your risk appetite.

Higher risk can be accepted into your portfolio when you are ready: you might start with higher dollar amount trades, multiple trades at the same time, or more complicated trading techniques.

Your Risk Tolerance

The key is to know your risk tolerance and stay within those boundaries. No one should force you to take on too much risk if it makes you feel uncomfortable. You might be 100 percent fine with day trading equities and ETFs. In fact, you might be so pleased with your returns for the amount of risk you are taking that you may never want to venture into the world of commodities, futures, or FX. Don't start to think that you are not a real day trader just because you have de-tuned your risk level to the point that you are enjoying your business, making money, and generally pleased with your results. Just because others seem to be suffering with their day trading efforts doesn't mean that they are more of a day trader than you. It may, in fact, be that the others who are having problems are expecting too much out of day trading; they may be trying complicated prepackaged commercial systems, or are trying to squeeze too much profit out of too small an account. Day trading should enhance your life, give you enjoyment, intellectual stimulation, and profit. It should not turn your world into a complicated mess of struggling with placing trades and then worrying about the potential effect on your account (and mental well-being!).

Keep it small and simple, and then if you would like, build up into a more risk-oriented structure in your account.

CHAPTER 19

Accounting and Taxes

If you are planning on doing any amount of day trading you will have to learn how to keep good records of the gains and losses in your account. You should also be keeping track of any expenses related to the production of your day trading income. These two numbers will allow you to arrive at your net income. When you use bookkeeping software, you can help your accountant simplify any tax planning she might advise.

Basic Record Keeping

You will do best when you keep a basic record of your day trading business's money inflows and outflows. A basic record can be a statement that can be kept in a notebook or on a spreadsheet such as Excel. If you have it in your plans to get an accountant for the formal preparation and assembly of your financial documents, your goal should be to make basic records of the cash ins and outs of your business.

What you are preparing is basic record keeping that is required for the preparation of an income statement. While you should record all of your expenses and income, you should also record the cash ins and outs related to the purchase of computer equipment, office furniture, and accounting and office-related software purchases. In addition to a record of these fixed asset purchases, you should record your additions and subtractions to your day trading accounts.

FACT

Modern accounting can trace it roots back to 1494 when a monk named Luca Pacioli wrote the first book on accounting. The book was called *Summa de Arithmetica, Geometria, Proportioni et Proportionalita*. With it came the advent of the notion of double entry bookkeeping. The book can still be found today in business schools across the country.

You should make a list of each cash outlay and income as they occur, with positive numbers representing cash income and negative numbers representing cash outflows and expenses. The first few lines would be the cash outflows related to the purchase of equipment and related costs. Each of these expenses would be recorded on a separate line with a description and the amount of the expenditure listed as a negative number. You would then take the receipt for the cash outflow and place it in an envelope.

At the start of each week you should label and start a new envelope, and place that week's expense and cash outflow receipts into that week's envelope.

The notebook should act as the main checking register of your day trading business. This means that even if you are out at the bookstore buying trading magazines and you spend money on coffee, and the money is cash, you would record the day, place, nature of expense (meals), and the cost of the item as a negative number.

If you start your day trading account with a $500, $5,000, or $50,000 deposit, you would record this in the book also as a negative number, as you "spent money" on the business. In fact, it is much like you "spent" $5,000, etc., on the opening of the account, an integral part of your day trading business. It is not exactly an expense, but it is money going out, and this is what you are trying to keep track of: money going out, and money coming in.

Recording Gains and Losses

In addition to the recording of the money flows in to and out of your account, you should record the gains and losses on your actual day trading activities. If you are making more than a few trades a day, the best way to record the gains and losses in your account is to make a record of the net gain and loss from your account on a daily basis. This can be done by writing down the value of your account before each trading session. This would be compared to the amount recorded on the closing of your last trading session. Any difference between the two would indicate the addition of interest that accrued from one trading session to the next. This interest should be recorded, separately, as interest is recorded separately on a U.S. tax return. After you take out this accumulated interest, the number you are left with is your actual trading session's starting amount.

As you trade throughout the day, you should keep track of the gains and losses that are generated with each trade. If you have a small amount of trades this can be easy to do, as you should be keeping records of your trading for review purposes. If you are doing many trades each session or you are engaging in trades that are retained from session to session such as an FX carry trade, or longer timeframe accumulation of a position, there is another method of recording gains and losses.

This alternate method is perfectly acceptable as far as the IRS is concerned and is often used in CPA tax preparation offices where the client is a heavy trader. In this method, your day trading account's value at the beginning of the trading session would be recorded, and after all of your trades were made, and your positions were opened and closed, you would record your day trading account's ending balance.

Make sure you are recording additions to and subtractions from your day trading account properly. If you don't identify them on your record, you will lose track of what is profit and what is an addition and subtractions of capital when you figure your books during tax time.

The account's ending balance would be subtracted from the beginning balance. The ending result would be your net gain or loss for that trading session. This daily gain or loss would be recorded in a separate book, labeled "Day Trading Gains/Losses per Session." Each session would be recorded on a separate line, with the date, amount of gain or loss, and the words "day trading, various."

The combined records of your expenses, money spent on fixed assets, deposits into and out of your day trading accounts, and the record of your daily day trading gains and losses make your record keeping complete. If you keep your gains/losses record and your cash record, you are going a long way in keeping your day trading business's overall profits and losses easy to keep track of, and ready for any formal document preparation.

Expenses, Net Income, and Taxes

Even though you will be recording your gains and losses from trading, what you are actually taxed on in the United States is your net income. This net income number is the difference of your net gains minus your expenses. If, for example, you have gains of $200, losses of $100, and expenses of $50, you have a net income of $50, and you will be taxed on this amount.

While your gains are pretty much set, as are your losses, the amount of your expenses is a key factor in your final net income number.

Common Expenses

These expenses can vary, but usually include the costs associated with the business use of your home, any mileage you might have incurred in the process of conducting business, the portion of utilities that are attributable to the operation of your day trading business, etc. Other expenses that can be used to reduce your overall net income include any subscription services, any meals out that were related to conducting business, and any travel (separate of your mileage amount) associated with your day trading business. Almost every cost associated with the establishment, upkeep, and conducting of your day trading business can be used as an expense on your income statement.

This income statement usually records the gains and losses from the beginning of the year to the end of the year at the top of the page. Below this are listed the categories of expenses related to the direct production of your day trading gains. Some of the categories are related to the business use of your home. This is usually calculated by measuring the total square footage of the home that is used exclusively for business purposes. This number is divided by the total square footage of the home. The resulting percentage is the amount of your rent expenses that can be assigned as a day trading business expense.

There are usually a large amount of expenses that can be attributed to your day trading business. You might be able to find some really good deductions if you consult one of the many guides to business expense deductions, including the IRS's website: *www.irs.gov/businesses.*

That same percentage is also taken for any shared utilities expenses, such as electric, heat, and water. Any repairs to the building would also be assigned to the business at this percentage, as would any condominium maintenance expenses. The key with finding what percentage of your home is used for business is to only use the square footage of the room or rooms that serve as your office space and are used for 100 percent business. There can be no dual-usage of these parts of the home. In other words, your office must be used exclusively for business, and not for personal reasons as well.

Phone Lines and Technology

Another key factor in determining if you own an actual business is if you have a phone line for the business that is separate from your personal line. Having a landline in your home fulfills the requirement of having a separate home phone, and your cell can then be used as your business line. The IRS also looks favorably on a business that has its own separate post office box as a sign that your endeavor is an actual business.

Other expenses include the depreciation of business equipment and software. While it is best to consult the tax code, generally any business funds that are spent on equipment are expensed and deducted over a period of several years. This deducting is called **depreciation expense** and the length of time and method of deduction can be determined by looking up the asset class in any number of tax guides that are available commercially.

The combination of your gains, losses, and related expenses result in what is called your net income. This net income number is the amount on which your business taxes will be based.

Tax Planning

Tax planning is the art of arranging your gains and expenses to arrive at a lower net income. This can best be achieved by matching up your gaining trades with a losing trade of equal or near equal value.

Matching Up Gains and Losses

For investors, this process can be done during the whole year, but when you are trading you have the advantage of matching up gains and losses with a shorter timeframe, ideally with the net effect of reducing your net gains on a daily basis. Matched gains and losses can be done on a weekly and monthly basis also. This matching is usually done by the closing out of positions that are on your books that are at a loss.

Normally, if you were building up a position for a long timeframe trade, you would hold on to the position and continue to buy into the security as it got to lower points during the trade's holding time. Holding the security and buying in on the dips would normally be your strategy; you might even be glad that the security fell into a loss for a short time as this would offer an opportunity to buy even more of the security at a lower price.

If you were following the tax planning method, you would weed out some of your longer-term trades that are currently losing. You would close them out at a loss if you determined that they would not turn around soon. To take tax planning further, you would make sure to do this at least once a quarter, and most of the closing out of these losing trades would be taken out in the week before the end of the quarter.

Cleaning House, Tax Planning, and Trades

"Cleaning house" would serve two purposes. The first would be to get the losing, non-performing trades off of your books with a certain time limit (quarterly). The second function would be to match your gains and losses at least once every quarter. This is important because if you are day trading full time, it is usually the custom to make quarterly estimated tax payments to the U.S. IRS. If you are matching your gains and losses, you would effectively be lowering your net income for each reportable quarter.

Corporations are a bit different from people and sole proprietorships. This is due to the fact that corporations usually have to be on an accrual basis of accounting. Still, the goal of tax planning for corporations is similar to that of individuals: to delay the recording of income for as long as possible while accelerating the recording of expenses.

On the other hand, your income statement consists of expenses as well as net gains. The goal of tax planning with your expenses is to accelerate your expenses so you can claim them sooner rather than later. This means that if you are planning a new computer purchase, software upgrade, or other investment in equipment, or thinking of incurring any other expenses, it would be beneficial to incur these expenses in an earlier reporting period rather than in a later period. This is true because expenses reduce your overall net income, and this reduction of net income translates to lower taxes.

To sum up, tax planning involves the reduction of your net gains by matching up your gains and losses. This matching up has the overall effect of lowering the first part of your income statement, the net gains section, and should be done at least once a quarter. Matching up your gains and losses once a quarter allows you to pay lower quarterly estimated income taxes. It also serves to weed out the non-performing trades on your books at least once every three months.

The second method of tax planning is to accelerate your expenses to the earliest tax period as possible, if economically feasible. This acceleration of expenses also has the effect of lowering your taxable income, as expenses are deducted from your gains to arrive at a net taxable income.

Bookkeeping Software

Introducing bookkeeping software into your day trading business will make it easier for you to sum up your gains, losses, and expenses at the end of each accounting period. Software programs such as Quicken and QuickBooks are affordable and easy to learn. Quicken and QuickBooks allow you to set up different income and expense categories. Once you set up the income and expense categories associated with your day trading business, it is easy to update the software with each and every transaction. You might choose to continue to keep a daily log of your day trading gains and losses in a spreadsheet program such as Microsoft's Excel and transfer the net amount of your gains and losses on a weekly basis.

This net gain from your day trading activities should be listed under a category called *trading gains* and would act much like an income account. If you had a net loss at week's end, this should be entered in an account called *trading losses*. This, too, is considered much like an income account.

Any expenses that you have recorded on a daily basis should be entered into your bookkeeping software at this time. Each type of expense would have a different account, from meals, to electric expense, to cable and Internet, to the predetermined percentage of your rent expense attributable to your business. Income and expenses have to be recorded with a minimum frequency of once a month. This once-a-month bookkeeping allows for the recording of the usual monthly expenses such as utilities, rent, etc.

Specialty Scanners

If you are keeping the receipts associated with your business, you can electronically record and store these also using specialty scanners. These scanners are small and come with data reading software. This data reading software reads the bar codes, date, store name, and dollar amount right off of the receipt when it is scanned. The scanned document will show up on the screen of your computer and the software will fill in the fields of a receipt information storage program with sections for all of the information usually required by the IRS. This information can then be saved. With some receipt scanning software the information can be directly uploaded to your bookkeeping software. Your bookkeeping software can then automatically read the information given to it by the scanning software. It will then fill in the sections of the expense accounts related to them.

Many bookkeeping software programs allow you to keep your records stored securely off site. If you choose this e-version of your software, your accountant can easily access your records with the sharing of an electronic passkey or key code. This would allow your accountant to conveniently look over your books without you having to visit her office.

Practice Good Bookkeeping

Good bookkeeping is essential to a well-running day trading business. Using bookkeeping software will help you get a grip on how profitable your business is, and will help out when you are preparing your own estimated quarterly and annual taxes, or if you choose, when you make your quarterly or annual trip to your accountant's office.

Getting an Accountant

Deciding to get an accountant can be a big step in your day trading business's development. Getting an accountant usually means that you are fully aware of the tax burden that successful day trading places upon your household. When you are a day trader and you are using brokerage accounts, you will get statements in the mail at least once a year. This statement will list the interest income the account has earned and the amount of the total sales of your account.

Shop around to find an accountant that you like. The business is very competitive, and you should be able to choose a professional that not only knows his business, but has a personality that agrees with yours. Most professionals charge similar hourly rates, giving you the choice as to whom you would like to retain for your tax advice.

Many brokerage firms do not provide a cost basis of your transactions. In other words, you will be sent a tax form at the end of the year that lists only the gross amount of the sales out of your account. If you are a frequent trader this amount can be as high as $500,000 or more. This amount is reported to the IRS as sales. By the IRS's viewpoint you made the $500,000 or more in income and you will be taxed on that amount. If, in fact, you made $500,000 in sales out of your account, but you made $450,000 in purchases to arrive at those sales, what you actually gained is $50,000.

The Benefits of Having an Accountant

The point is, without a cost basis reported to the IRS, the burden of proving your actual gain on those sales rests on you. There has been more than one time that someone has filed and paid their taxes, only to get a letter from the IRS that a point is open as to the additional sales proceeds as shown by their broker. If you are not keeping good records of your cost basis, you would have a difficult time correcting this matter.

The employment of an accountant can help rectify this matter, as accountants, CPAs, and tax attorneys know the key points in making a proper income statement, and all of the documentation that goes into making a properly filed tax return. You might even use an accountant to keep your books, in a form of taking the bookkeeping process out of your hands from the point of expense and income recording. You could keep your Excel- or paper-based records as you normally would, but employ an accountant's office to record them on QuickBooks once a month. This would be a cost-effective measure, as most accountants would go over your records at the end of the year anyway when they looked for errors. In this way your bookkeeping could be done right the first time.

Other Benefits

If you used a CPA firm, you could also have them file your quarterly estimated income tax payments, which is something that not everyone is comfortable doing themselves.

Other benefits to seeking the help of a CPA or tax attorney is the access to advanced tax planning knowledge, the setting up of a retirement plan for tax benefits, and to have access to a business consultant that is specially trained in the tax matters of day traders.

You can find tax professionals who specialize in the tax matters of day traders by asking your current attorney, private banker, or family CPA. Not every CPA and attorney has the specialized knowledge required for your day trading business. It is best to ask around and find one that does. Tax attorney and CPA fees are usually high, but worth every penny come tax time.

CHAPTER 20

Making Day Trading Your Job

In order to get to the point that you are able to make day trading your job, you will first have to get into the idea of building up an account and keep developing your skills. Next, you will have to develop a budget that will give you the financial flexibility to keep trading while you are slowly going pro. Lastly, by defining your ultimate goals of day trading, you can live the day trading lifestyle.

The Philosophy of Building Up an Account

In order to get to the point that you can make day trading your job, you need to be able to make enough money from day trading to draw a salary against. In order to do this you will need to have enough money in your day trading account to make a number of big enough trades to throw off large dollar profits.

Adding Funds Regularly

When you are starting out, a smaller account balance will do just fine, and in some aspects is recommended. Smaller accounts are easier to manage and easier to deal with psychologically, as it can be a daunting task to set up a series of really big trades. Once you get the gist of reading the markets, looking for setups, and placing trades of smaller amounts, you will most likely want to develop your trading into more positions of larger size. To do this you will have to build up the balance of your day trading account.

Building up an account can be done in two ways: the first through gains, and the second by adding funds from an outside source. Adding funds from an outside source can build up your account very quickly, and is usually the most controllable. If you are interested in the building up of your account by adding funds, you must find a source of funds that is steady, and can be set aside for day trading. If you are day trading part time, and still have a source of income outside of trading, you could use this income as your source. If you get paid bi-weekly or monthly, you could deposit a certain amount into your day trading account with every pay period. If you are collecting a pension or are receiving any sort of regular income, this too could be part of your source for adding to your day trading account.

Look for Ways to Set Money Aside

The secret is that if you want to build up your account, you should look for ways in which to set aside money for that purpose. If you find that day trading is something that you are good at, find enjoyable, and find profitable, perhaps it is time for you to channel some of your funds away from the other forms of spending options you may have.

For example, if you allow yourself a certain amount of money for personal use each week, perhaps some of this money could be directed to your day trading account. It is a matter of setting priorities with your extra money. If you would normally use extra money for personal wants, perhaps you could cut back on fun expenditures, and instead put the money in your day trading account.

Remember, while you might really want to build up your account in a hurry, by no means over-sacrifice in order to direct money into your day trading business. The key is to add to your account as you can, and spend time searching for ways to add money comfortably.

There are stories of people who wanted a trading account so badly that they put a quarter of their income into their account. These people found it so profitable to day trade that they knew that if they wanted to make the transition from working for someone to working full time at day trading that they would have to have a large account balance. You too can make as many deposits as necessary to your account to build it up to the point you need it to be at to day trade for a living.

Developing Skills

Developing the skills required to read the market, analyze the charts, and look for setups takes time. It also takes time to learn how to manage your cash and margin, and to develop the technical skills needed for smooth order entries. Try not to be too impatient in the accumulation of your skills over time. It takes four years to go through college to develop the skills required for a career, and longer if you go to graduate school. It will not, of course, take this long to train and develop the skills required for successful day trading. It might take several seasons, though. This is because it takes months for certain scenarios in the market to fully work out, and it is often very beneficial to see a situation as it develops from beginning to end. It will also take you time to learn to spot trends as they are developing, and have the ability to compare them with trends that you might have noticed from your previous trading sessions.

Acquiring Skills Over Time

Developing your skills should bc a process that lasts your entire day trading career. It starts with reading all you can about the markets and progresses on to a casual review of the market news at the end of your day.

When will I know that I am really "into" day trading?
You know you are really into day trading when your day revolves around the market's open, and when you feel as though you can't rest until the market closes. You also know you're absorbing the day trading lifestyle when you wake up and immediately check the overnight market news.

Your skill development will come naturally as you are trading, day in and day out. You will get good at listening to the news, spotting trends, and looking for setups. The sheer number of transactions that you will place over the weeks and months will add up to a regular day trading academy. If you are planning your trades, building positions, and reviewing these trades after they have been closed out, you are ensuring a process of a daily examination of your experiences of day trading. The more you trade, the easier it will become. You will also naturally find yourself shying away from marginal trades and only going after building positions that have a high degree of success. Couple this with the natural dwelling on the markets and day trading in general and you have created a very good training and learning environment for success.

Keep Practicing

As long as you continue to be profitable, and your day trading endeavors pay for themselves, then you are good to go—no matter how long it takes for you to feel as though you have mastered the subject. Keep placing, thinking about the market, searching for solutions to your questions, and day trading in both your live and practice accounts, and it will all come together. Soon you will find yourself feeling confident of your skills, able to enter and exit out of trades at a profit, and draw a salary against your account.

Slowly Going Pro

If your goal is to at some point quit your full-time job and day trade full time, then what you need to do is set a financial plan. If you are working on developing your day trading skills while working, so much the better, as you are in the position to not be forcing your account to earn too high a return. This forcing of an account to earn too high a return can often result in taking too high a risk/reward ratio in your trades. Too high a risk/reward ratio can lead to an account losing trades, and in the worst case, the eventual closing out of all of your accounts, resulting in the end of your day trading experience. If you are still working while day trading and giving yourself enough time to develop skills and work through ideas in your demo account, then you most likely have the opportunity to build up a savings account outside of your day trading account.

If your plans are to start day trading professionally, then build yourself a plan that outlines the steps required to get you to the point that you can make the break and go into day trading full time. Goals are best made by writing them down in steps, and marking them off as you complete them.

Building a Savings Account

If your goal is to go pro, and live the day trading lifestyle, then you will need a healthy savings account to give you a form of a security blanket. It is often said that you need three to six months worth of salary in a money market or laddered CDs in order to have a free mind and a secure feeling about your finances. This is the standard number of months' worth of savings when you are still in the working world, and drawing a steady paycheck. When you are about to begin a career of day trading and are away from the security of a paycheck, you too will need a savings account built up.

This savings account has to 100 percent separate from your day trading account, and should never overlap. A savings account is there for you when things go bad, or when you have to cover a shortfall in your monthly draw out of your account due to a slower trading month. A good rule of thumb is to figure into your budget not being able to make a draw out of your account for at least six to nine months straight. With this in mind, you would need to have a minimum of twelve months living expenses saved up.

Keep in mind that this is not the same as twelve months salary saved. Your previous salary and your actual living expenses are usually quite different. Before you begin your full-time trading career it makes sense to really get an idea of what you actually need, as far as income, to keep your household running. Also, with a bit of planning, you could wait to go pro until a major monthly expense is paid off, such as when your car is fully paid for, etc. The goal is to give yourself as much a chance of surviving economically without the benefit of large draws from your account. This might mean scaling down your expenses, and refraining from a few luxuries. You must decide what you can live with and without to get to the point where you are a full-time day trader.

You should never figure in your retirement accounts when you are deciding where you are going to find sources of funds to help you start day trading full time. Retirement accounts such as 401k and IRA money should never be thought of as a backup source of funds for your day trading business.

More about Budgeting

In order to be a full-time day trader you will need to be able to withstand several months at a time where you are not drawing a salary against your day trading account. In order to do this you will have to develop a workable budget of what your monthly and quarterly expenses are. If you would like to go pro but you find it hard to save up enough money to have twelve months in reserve, then it is perfectly acceptable to trade in three-quarter time, and have the added security of working at a low-impact, part-time job.

You might find it useful to have a sideline consulting business, where you are able to supplement your day trading income by the occasional technological or business gigs. This is actually a good way of ensuring your success in the day trading business, as it always seems to happen that you land a big account when the world's markets are closing up for the season. Sure, it would be nice to be a full-time trader, but the real goal is to trade, no matter what the circumstances. If this means working the two to get to where you want to be, then you have arrived at a solution. In fact, this is often what many traders do to get their accounts built, all the while having the freedom to leave their full-time jobs.

Getting to that point all revolves around a budget. If you find that you need $4,000 a month to get by, bare minimum, then perhaps you could supply your needs with $1,500 in a day trading draw, $1,500 in savings, and $1,000 in a monthly part-time consulting business.

ESSENTIAL

Everyone's goals and reasons to be successful with day trading are different. Yours might be as simple as having a source of extra money. They may be a bit more complex, such as some day traders getting into the business and day trading as a form of sport.

If you really want to day trade full time, you will have to sit down and find a way to fund your dreams. If you work on your budget, you will find sources of income and ways to keep your expenses down, which gets you to the point where things work out and you are day trading full time.

Defining Your Ultimate Goals for Day Trading

If you set out in day trading with a plan in mind, you have a greater chance of getting to where you want to go. Think of some of the reasons of why you wanted to get into day trading in the first place. Whatever the reasons, you should remind yourself of these goals. If your goal is to day trade FX at night, and make enough in your account to pay some bills at the end of the month, then keep those goals in mind, and be especially happy when that time comes.

There are many benefits to day trading, from knowing about the markets, to earning a living, to feeling the enjoyment of playing the market. Day trading should be run like a business you own. Like any business you would own, it serves its purpose when it works for you, and fulfills your financial needs. Unlike some business types, though, day trading can be done at your home office, or anywhere, and at practically anytime.

Living the Day Trading Lifestyle

When you are day trading you're living one of the best working lifestyles in the world. You are in the league of the traders from investment banks and hedge funds all over the globe. From the traders working at their desks at the vast trading departments of major international banks, to small three and four man hedge funds based out of Geneva, Switzerland—trading is big business, and many people would like to get in on the action.

At the end of the trading session, only you will determine what it means to be living the day trading lifestyle. It may mean spending more time with your kids, being able to take a day off whenever you like, or having the chance to follow your dreams of building up a big bank account.

If you have the opportunity to learn the business from the ground up by studying the markets and starting small, you too have the ability to develop your own trading style. Your personal trading style and goals can lead you to day trading casually when the market suits you, to having a full-fledged business. If you develop your trading skills to the point where you are day trading profitably and consistently, you could also allow yourself to rely on your day trading gains as a source of income. When you get to the point where you are making your first salary draws against your account, you are entering the big time.

Many people want to be successful at investing, and many more want to be successful at day trading. There is glamour to winning in the market and making profit by quickly moving money into and out of securities. Being successful in day trading carries a mystique with it. The day trading lifestyle is one to be admired, but when you're successful at it, it will seem like the most natural thing.

APPENDIX A

Glossary

2 percent rule
A method of building in stop-loss settings (automatic closing of a position) to limit the overall loss of a position to 2 percent of the cash balance of your total day trading account.

American Depository Receipt (ADR)
An ADR is a share of stock that is directly tied to the price of a share of stock of a company that is listed on a non-U.S. exchange.

Annual report
An audited listing of a publicly traded company's financial statements and statements to shareholders.

Arbitrage
The buying and selling of securities on different exchanges at the same instant in an attempt to gain on the price difference between the two markets.

Arms index
Attempts to read the conditions of the stock market by looking at the number of shares on the NYSE that have fallen and risen and the volume of these shares.

Asset valuation
A method of determining the value of property or claims on property without the actual sale of the property. To arrive at an effective valuation, the two pieces of property must be similar in nature, quality, and quantity.

Available margin
A form of a credit card for buying stock or other tradable sector.

Balance sheet

A financial document that shows the assets, liabilities, and owner's equity of a business. A balance sheet is divided into two parts; the asset side must equal the liability and equity side.

Bear market

A market condition when the investor's and trader's risk sentiment is low; also when a market is falling in overall price.

Beta (ß)

A measure of a securities' volatility in relation to the overall market. A beta of 1.0 would indicate the security moves in tandem with the market, while a beta of 2.0 would indicate the security's movement is twice as volatile as the overall market.

Basis point

The commission in FX accounts, equal to .01 percent.

Big Mac Index

A term coined by the publishers of the periodical *The Economist. The Economist* publishes their version of a PPP measurement by recording the cost of a McDonald's Big Mac in several countries around the world. The thought is that the Big Mac is a good measure of PPP, as it is the same commodity worldwide.

Book entry format

Accounting entries made to record the transfer of gold reserves from vault to vault.

Bourses
A European term for a trading area, usually where financial products, art or numismatics are traded in an organized exchange-like arena.

Bretton Woods system
Financial system in which the U.S. dollar was linked to gold. Foreign nations could easily exchange the dollars they had in reserve for the gold that was held in the vaults of the U.S. government.

Broker
The financial intermediary required in order to trade securities. A firm that holds trading and investing accounts for clients.

Bubble in the market
A condition of securities that are greatly overpriced due to ease of credit, allowing greater and greater price expansion in the market.

Bull market
A market where there is an overall good feeling; usually indicated by rising prices over an extended time.

Buy and hold
An investment strategy that uses security selection as its main requirement; usually for longer timeframe investors.

Buy on the dips
A method of allocating a certain amount of your portfolio to one security and adding to your position of this security when the price naturally hits low points throughout the trading horizon.

Capital gain

The money made on an investment when the sales price is higher than the purchase price.

Capitalization

The sum of the long-term debt and the stock in the set up of a company. This is often called the structure of the company, and the amount of debt in relation to the amount of equity in the company will tell you how conservatively the company is structured; the lower the amount of debt, the more conservative.

Carry trades

Trading long, high-yielding currencies versus low-yielding currencies.

Cash flow

A measurement of the inflows and outflows through a company for a given length of time.

CBOE Volatility Index

An intraday index; its main use is as an indicator of traders' and investors' emotional feelings about the market. The higher the VIX number is, the greater the negative feelings in the market. A normal reading is anywhere from 15 to 25. Also known as the VIX Index.

Certificate of Deposit (CD)

A financial product sold by a bank that operates much like a savings account, only with a maturation date.

Coffers
A term from the Italian Renaissance referring to the chest in money traders and banker's vaults that held the actual gold and silver coinage.

Combination brokerage firms
Firms that have trained licensed brokers available to assist in the setting up of a trade or a hedge trade. They have two types of pricing structures, one for online trading at the discount rate, and one for broker-assisted trades, at a higher, full-service rate.

Commodity
Any raw materials that are fully interchangeable and uniform and used in the manufacture of processed goods.

Commodity currencies
Currencies of commodity-producing economies.

Deep-discount firms
These brokerages will offer a discount on the price if you exceed a certain amount of trades, usually above fifty in a monthly period.

Defensive cash account
The mindset that your cash account is the source of your paycheck and the source of a day trading business's self sufficiency. You should get to the point that your day trading business is completely self-sufficient and in no way harms your total picture of economic well-being.

Depreciation expense

A deduction allowed by the IRS that spreads the cost of fixed assets over an assigned lifespan of three, five, or seven years depending on the classification of the equipment or fixed asset.

Discount firm

Discount firms offer the same back office, order entry, and market access as a full-service firm. The only difference is that you will not have a representative to speak with, and most likely the discount firm will not offer its own research, but will rely on outside sources for this critical information instead.

Dollar cost averaging

Buying at regular intervals, at high points of the market and at low points of the market.

Dow Theory

A method used to plot the future movement of a security using the Dow Jones industrial 30 average and the Dow Jones transportation averages as base lines.

Earnings per share (EPS)

Found by taking the net earnings and dividing it by the total number of shares outstanding. The relative value of the market as a whole, measured by comparing the ratio of the S&P 500 average earnings per share to the percentage yield of a ninety-day U.S. government T-bill.

Earnings season

During earnings season, companies can exceed or miss what the market expected their profits to be, and this can lead to exaggerated and unpredictable price movements in a stock's price.

Elliott Wave Theory
Employs past information of a security movement to predict the securities future direction. The basis is that securities in the market have five distinct steps, and these steps form three separate waves. The theory is that once all of the five of the different parts of the wave have worked their way through, a top (or bottom) is in play. When a top or bottom is reached, this also marks the beginning of a fresh trend.

E-mini futures contracts
Futures contracts that are structured much like the full-sized contracts, except the they have much smaller lot sizes. Because they have smaller lot sizes, they are easier to manage, and it is easier to have multiple positions in your account at any one time.

Endowments
Often referred to as "institutional investors" or "institutional money." These funds are associated with colleges, nonprofit groups, and other asset holders that have set aside assets that are to be separate from the day to day activities of the group, and are held to be professionally and actively managed for stability and gain.

Entry points
The point at which you make your initial purchase of a stock, commodity, or currency.

Equity
The part of a company that is owned, as opposed to debt.

Euro
The name of the common currency of the European Union. It is also known as EUR or €.

Exchange traded funds (ETFs)
A security that trades intraday much like a stock, but holds a basket of underlying securities that influences its price and movement.

Floating rate system
Meaning that exchange rates are not set; however, they might have a target amount set by the central bank of the country or economic entity that issues them.

Foreign exchange trading
The act of going into the electronic or interbank market to trade the money of other nations by selling one currency and using the proceeds to buy another currency. Profit is made when the prices of the two currencies move in a favorable direction in relation to the opening trade.

Forwards
Much like a future—a contract is signed to buy a financial asset in the future at a set price, but in the case of forwards, the contract is custom made between the parties and is not freely tradable on an exchange.

Full-service brokerage firm
Firms that offer overall market technical analysis, sector and industry-specific analysis, and information regarding the trading potential of the S&P 500, ETFs, commodities, and currencies as to where to place enter and exit points during your trading day.

Full-service firm
Opening an account with a full-service firm will give you access to a licensed representative who is trained in securities selection and the setting up of trades. Most full-service firms allow you to trade almost all classes of

securities from equities to futures to foreign exchange, and can also offer competitive interest rates on the unused cash portion of your portfolio.

Futures contract
A derivative financial instrument whose value is tied to the expected price of an underlying asset at a set time in the future.

FX account
A brokerage account that allows the holder to trade in the foreign exchange markets, buying and selling the world's currencies.

Going long
A term used to state you have a trade that is set up to make money when the security or sector is moving upward.

Going public
The efforts involved and the act of raising capital for a company for the first time in the capital markets through the issue of an initial public offering or IPO.

Going short
A trade that is structured to produce a profit when the underlying security loses value.

Hard assets
See raw materials.

Hedging
The act of using multiple strategies or multiple positions to reduce the overall risk in an investment or trading portfolio.

Hedge fund
An investment company that uses multiple positions and high degrees of leverage to achieve high levels of returns while minimizing risk.

Hot market
The secret of getting into a security before a bubble collapses.

Income statement
Found within an annual report. Shows sales, expenses, and net income; this is shown over a twelve-month period.

Independent investor
An independent investor usually has a buy and hold strategy of selecting securities and holding them for the long term.

Independent trader
Independent traders are the group of people who day trade in their privately held accounts with their private money. They are the only ones to share in the profits derived from day trading.

Initial public offering
Usually the first attempt by a successful privately held company to raise cash for expansion by selling shares of itself to institutional investors and the public.

Intervening in the markets
When governments or central banks attempt to regulate the value of their currencies. This is done by the government or central bank buying or selling its own currency in the inter-bank market in an attempt to force a change in value of that currency.

Investment banker
Someone who analyzes a company, performs all background checks, and prepares a company for an IPO.

Investment banks
A financial services company or partnership that offers corporate finance advice, financing, brokerage accounts, and IPO services as its main line of business.

In play
A stock (or other investment) is in play when some news has come out on the company, and the news has caused other traders to take notice. When other traders take notice, a stock will go up or down, depending on whether the news is perceived to be good or bad for the company.

Japanese candlestick charts
Charts that read much like bar charts—the main difference is what is reported on the chart. The high and low for the day, and the opening and closing price of the day are shown. Also, there is a difference in the charts for when the end of the day price is lower than the beginning of the day price, and vice versa.

Letter to shareholders
Found within an annual report; tells the nature of the business operation.

Letter to stockholders
Found within an annual report. Tells you how the company has been doing and where they would like to go in the future.

Leverage
The use of credit as a multiplier for the purchase of a security. Also known as gearing.

Liabilities
The short-term and long-term debts of a company.

Long-only trades
A trade where the stock or ETF gains in value when the price of the stock or ETF goes up in value.

Long-term perspectives
Day trading timeframes of three to six months that rely heavily upon fundamental analysis as well as technical chart evaluations.

Margin
The amount of the credit balance that a client has in his brokerage account.

Margin accounts
Where you put in a certain amount of cash and the brokerage firm supplies you with a credit card–like balance that is able to give you additional buying power—some margin amounts are limited by regulation, such as stocks and futures.

Margin call
This could happen if you used the margin in your account like a credit card to purchase the ETF and the value of the position fell far enough to require you to either close out the position and pay back the margin you borrowed, or have the option of depositing more money in your account to be above the required amount. Margin calls are looked upon as unfavorable and can be very disruptive to trading.

Market cap
The number of shares outstanding in the market times the price of the share.

Market chatter
Short-term news reports.

Market regulators
Regulators that are in control as to what amount of margin is able to be used in stock, ETF, and futures accounts.

Market reports
Sources that offer a logical view of the market. They are often based on mathematics, past market activity, market fundamentals, and technical indicators.

McClellan Overbought/Oversold Oscillator
Measures the velocity of the money moving in to and out of the markets, and is calculated for the NYSE and the NASDAQ.

Modern Portfolio Theory
The concept of limiting risk and enhancing reward, first introduced by Harry Markowitz. In 1952, Markowitz mathematically proved that risk could

be reduced by the movement away from single securities and toward the inclusion of non-correlated securities into the portfolio.

Momentum
The measure of a security's rate of movement.

Money supply indicator
Calculated by starting with 100 and adding the percent change in M2, and subtracting the percent change in the Consumer Price Index.

Moving average deviation
Calculated by dividing the security's last price by its ten-week moving average.

Multiple-sector account
Brokerage accounts that usually have a higher minimum then the pure FX accounts, as the "lot size" in the other sectors might require a higher minimum to trade effectively.

Mutual funds
An investment vehicle that is comprised of a basket of securities and offers the diversification benefits of an ETF, but has its price calculated only once a day, at the close of the markets.

Net long
Over time, an average of more long positions than short positions.

Net profit on a trade
The amount realized from a transaction, minus the transaction fees, minus the price of entry, leaving the overall profit on the trade.

Offensive cash account
A philosophy of entering and exiting trades with the thought of increasing net worth, no matter how small the gain might be.

Offshore brokers
International investment firms. One can invest in foreign stocks, foreign indexes, and the indexes of developing parts of the world.

Options' trading
Often considered the most risky form of trading due to the time element of the options. This time element means that as the days progress toward the expiration date of an options contract, they are worth less and less, to the point of having zero time value, only intrinsic value.

Order entry
The method that an online trading terminal uses to actually purchase or sell a security.

Pension funds
See Endowments.

P/E ratio
A fundamental analysis tool; its formula is share price/earnings per share.

Perfect hedge
A position that is hedged to the point that the risk has been eliminated. In theory, a perfect hedge eliminates all risk, but at the same time eliminates the possibility of any return.

Philosophy of buy and hold
A passive investment technique of buying carefully selected securities, buying them and holding them for the long term, usually to reap long-term capital gains at a tax-advantaged rate.

PIPs
In an FX account, basis points commissions.

Pivot point
When a security travels past its support or resistance point with a lot of volume, it is thought to be a good breakout. The point of the breakout is called a pivot point, and is often followed by a test of the breakout, a time when the market rethinks the breakout, and the security falls in price.

Position
Your position is when you make a case for the trade and start building it.

Position trading
A method of building up more and more inventory of a security over time, often a month or longer, with a clear selling price point in mind.

Price discovery
Going into the open market to find the going rate for the price of a security.

Price setting
Finding out the going rate of an item that is to be transacted.

Priced in
When the market builds the expected positive or negative news into the value of their trades and positions.

Primary market
A place where companies can come to market and raise money for their businesses.

Profit taking
When traders sell off a security after it reaches a psychologically important level.

Proprietary trading
The term referring to when a firm trades its own company-owned money in-house for their own profit, and not for a client's account.

Purchasing power parity (PPP)
A measurement of the misevaluation of the same goods from country to country as measured in a base currency, such as the U.S. dollar.

Pyramiding (the pyramid method)
Pyramiding is entering and exiting trades with three equal dollar amounts in order to smooth your average position cost and selling price. This buying and selling method is a form of safe position management.

Quantitative easing
When banks can intervene in the currency markets to force the adjustment of their currency.

Raw materials
Any one of the asset classes that are based on a physical asset such as oil, copper, corn, and lumber.

Read the fundamentals
The process of knowing the economic or financial statements of a country, market, sector, or security.

Resistance level
A psychologically important level in a security's or index's chart, often very resistant to breach due to the world's traders all making the same assumption of the securities price.

Risk-free rate
The benchmark interest rate number of a totally liquid and risk-free security, commonly measured by the ninety-day U.S. T-bill rate.

Risk management
A method of using mathematics and hedging to build a model and implementing methods of limiting risk while maximizing the potential for returns in a trading portfolio.

Scalping
Trading using a five to ten minute timeframe.

Secondary market
Once a stock is sold for the first time, it then enters this market.

Security-selection approach
An analysis when you are looking at the big picture and using fundamentals.

Security-timing approach
Relying on the timing and price level of a security to determine the proper entry and exit point of a trade.

Shorting
A term used to state you have a trade that is set up to make money when the security or sector is moving downward.

Short interest indicator
A report that shows the amount of shares that are held on the short sale side of investors and traders, representing the number of traders who think the market will go down from its current level.

Short-term perspective
The time it takes to evaluate the day's market conditions and news, look for setups, and commit to a trade.

Statement of cash flows
Shows how money flowed in, out, and through a company during the same year as the income statement.

Stochastic
The measurement in percentage terms of the price velocity of an individual security or market index as compared to a range set by a technician.

Stockholder's equity
A representation of the difference between what the company owns and what it owes.

Stocks
An ownership share of a company.

Stop
Where the trading platform will automatically sell when it reaches a certain point.

Stop-loss order
When you precalculate the maximum loss you would take in the trade before your trading platform places an automated closing out of the trade, thereby placing a limit on the percentage and dollar amount of the potential loss of the trade.

Support and resistance of the security
When you draw a line at the average bottom price and top price, you find the support and resistance of a security.

Swaps
A custom made contract is entered into with the obligation of both parties to trade securities (usually FX) at the beginning of the contract and return like securities back to the original owners at the end of the term by "re-swapping" the exact or like securities.

Synergy of the business
How a business's customers are better served by the company operating as a whole unit, as well as the value of their repeat customers.

Take-profit order
When you enter in beforehand the amount of profit in percentage or dollar amount that you would like to make on the trade. When the security meets the price level that is required to meet your preset profit amount, your trading platform will automatically close out the position, and lock in your gains.

Tax planning
The art of arranging your gains and expenses to arrive at a lower net income.

Technical analysis
A system of reading charts off a computer screen. Looks at the supply and demand data as presented by indicators.

The time in the trade
The length that you, as the trader, are holding the stock, exchange traded funds (ETF), or commodity.

Top-down approach
The process of starting with the big picture, looking at a country's economy, a particular sector, a security, and then switching to technical analysis to make the final decision as to a possible entry and exit point.

Total return strategy
The returns of your account are the combined interest accrual, and the added boost of trading gains is the true measure of your accounts performance. This combined number is often called a total return strategy.

Trading platform
Trading software.

Tranches
Large orders to be placed with institutional investors. Tranches are often bundled together to have the same financial characteristics, and are often sold in units of $1 million or more per order.

Trusted sources
Sources that will tell you the direction in which the market is likely to be going in the future. These are usually the longer timeframe reports and market summaries that are published by your broker.

Uncorrelated diversification
In your day trading portfolio, when you have different positions spread across many securities, industries, and markets, so that when one trade turns bad, it is supported by many others that are not related or affected by that trading/market event or news.

Unrealized gains
The profits are still "on paper" and not yet in the day trader's account, as the trade has not been closed out yet.

Unrealized profit or loss
The profit or loss that you would make on a trade if you closed the trade at that exact moment.

VIX Index
See CBOE Volatility Index.

Wash sale
The sale of a security at a loss thirty days before or after the purchase of the same security. Any losses from a wash sale are disallowed according to IRS regulations.

Weekly average profit
A measure of your profits that smoothes out the natural daily ups and downs of the trading week. Gains are netted with losses, giving a weekly net gain or loss.

Weighted average cost of capital (WACC)
The formula used to find the balance between debt and equity on a company's balance sheet. The WACC varies upon the cost of debt and the tax bracket of the corporation.

WST ratio
An indicator that uses information derived from options traders.

Zero-based
A term referring to the settling of profits and losses between accounts at the end of each trading day; used in the futures markets to prevent account holders from getting too deeply in the negative with their individual trades.

APPENDIX B

Additional Resources

Books

Andresky, Fraser. *The Business Owner's Guide to Personal Finance: When Your Business Is Your Paycheck.* (Princeton, NJ: Bloomberg Press, 2002).

Archer, Michael D. *Getting Started in Currency Trading: Winning in Today's Forex Market.* (Hoboken, NJ: John Wiley & Sons, 2010).

Bernstein, Jacob. *How the Futures Markets Work: Understanding The Fastest Game in Town.* (Paramus, NJ: NYIF/New York Institute of Finance, 2000).

Bernstein, Peter L. *The Power of Gold: The History of an Obsession.* (New York: John Wiley & Sons, 2000).

Bernstein, Peter L. *Against the Gods: The Remarkable Story of Risk.* (New York, NY: John Wiley & Sons, 1996).

Burgess, Gareth. *Trading and Investing in the Forex Market Using Chart Techniques.* (Hoboken, NJ: John Wiley & Sons, 2009).

Downes, John, and Jordan Elliot Goodman. *Barron's Finance & Investment Handbook.* (Hauppauge, NY: Barron's Educational Series, 2007).

Ferguson, Niall. *The House of Rothschild.* (New York, NJ: Viking, 1998–1999).

Kleinman, George. *Trading Commodities and Financial Futures: A Step-by-Step Guide to Mastering the Markets.* (Boston, MA: Financial Times Press, 2005).

Kline, Donna. *Fundamentals of the Futures Market.* (New York, NY: McGraw-Hill, 2001).

Lefèvre, Edwin. *Reminiscences of a Stock Operator.* (Hoboken, NJ: John Wiley & Sons, 2006).

Rosenstreich, Peter. *Forex Revolution: An Insider's Guide to the Real World of Foreign Exchange Trading.* (Indianapolis, IN: Financial Times Prentice Hall Books, 2005).

Economic and Financial News Sources

Barron's
The online version of the financial news magazine. Includes financial and stock investing news, rankings and reports, and market data.
http://online.barrons.com

ClearStation.com
"The intelligent investment community." A very technical website through E*Trade, providing up-to-the-minute information on stocks and markets.
http://clearstation.etrade.com

CNBC
Breaking financial news and information on markets and all things economics.
www.cnbc.com

Dailystocks.com
Provides charting, market commentary, news, and fundamental research for U.S. stocks.
www.dailystocks.com

The Economist
Web access is available to the weekly magazine. Check out the Economics focus articles.
www.economist.com

Federal Reserve Bank of New York
The New York Federal Reserve Bank's daily breakdown on the entire economy is a must for anyone in need of the latest economic news. The PDF file includes graphs and charts on the entire economy and is updated daily. Used daily by the author.
www.newyorkfed.org/research/directors_charts/econ_fin.pdf

Moody's Economy.com
"Moody's Analytics is a leading independent provider of economic, financial, country, and industry research designed to meet the diverse planning and information needs of businesses, governments, and professional investors worldwide."
www.economy.com

The Motley Fool
Investing information, top news stories, stock and investing tips videos, opinions, and much more.
www.fool.com

MSN Investor
Financial and economic news, plus information on markets, stocks, funds, ETFs, and brokers.
http://moneycentral.msn.com/investor/home.asp

The Wall Street Journal
The official website of the *Wall Street Journal* newspaper, featuring business news and financial news. Includes coverage of breaking news and current headlines from the U.S. and around the world.
http://online.wsj.com

Yahoo! Finance
Includes up-to-date financial news from around the world, as well as investing and personal finance information. Also features special tools for building and managing portfolios.
http://finance.yahoo.com

Other Websites

Bank of England
www.bankofengland.co.uk

Bank for International Settlements
www.bis.org

Central Bank Website Listings
www.bis.org/cbanks

Bank of Japan
www.boj.or.jp/en

CME Group
www.cmegroup.com

Deutche Bank USA
www.db.com/usa

European Central Bank
www.ecb.int

InvestorsEurope
www.investorseurope.com

Kitco Base Metals
www.kitcometals.com

Kitco Gold & Precious Metals
www.kitco.com

Kitco Silver
www.kitcosilver.com

The London Bullion Market Association
www.lbma.org.uk

London Metal Exchange
www.lme.com

Merrill Lynch International
www.ml.com

Monetary Authority of Singapore
www.mas.gov.sg

Norges Bank
www.norges-bank.no

OANDA fxTrade
http://fxtrade.oanda.com

Reserve Bank of Australia
www.rba.gov.au

Reserve Bank of New Zealand
www.rbnz.govt.nz

The Riksbank
www.riksbank.com

SW Consulting
Directory of Swiss Banks
www.swconsult.ch/cgi-bin/banklist.pl

Stock, Futures, and Options
www.sfomag.com

The Swiss National Bank
www.snb.ch

UBS Global Homepage
www.ubs.com

U.S. Bureau of Economic Analysis
www.bea.gov

U.S. Department of the Treasury
www.ustreas.gov

U.S. Federal Reserve
www.federalreserve.gov

World Gold Council
www.gold.org

APPENDIX C

What to Trade When

You might ask yourself, "What do I trade at this particular time?" You might also observe that the market has been in a downturn for some time and that it is due for a reversal. The conditions might be the exact opposite. There might have been three days or even a week of up days in the market, and you feel as though that the world's traders will engage in "taking some money off of the table," or profit taking. When this happens they will sell some of their positions and the market will go down. How do you prepare for this and possibly make some money on well-placed trades? What you have to do is look for setups in the market.

Potential Setups in the Markets

When the market is expected to move in one direction (usually after a run up or a downturn that lasts some time), there are a few trades that usually work well.

POTENTIAL FX TRADES FOR EXPECTED TURNS IN THE MARKET

Short the Commodity Currencies versus the Lower-Yielding Currencies for a Downturn in the Market

Short AUD/USD

Short NZD/USD

Short CAD/USD

Long USD/NOK

Short AUD/JPY

Short NZD/JPY

Short CAD/JPY

Short AUD/CHF

Short NZD/CHF

Short CAD/CHF

Long CHF/NOK

Shorting of the commodity currencies against the lower-yielding currencies works well because the commodity currencies (the currencies of the nations that produce commodities for export as their main source of income) are often high-yield currencies. This means that the interest rates on the commodity currencies are often 3 percent, 4 percent, or even 5 percent or greater than the other currency in the pair. When this happens, the lower-yielding currency is considered to be a "risky asset" as compared to the lower-yielding currency, whether it is the CHF, the JPY, or the USD.

Question: Why do these trades usually work?

Answer: When conditions in the market contract, or when there seems to be a pull back in the market, the world's traders will rush to the lower-yielding currencies in favor of the higher-yielding "risky" currencies due to the perceived lower risk of the lower-yielding currencies. Traders will rush into the relative safety of these low-yielding currencies and will often call them "safe-haven currencies."

Another good FX play when the market is expected to downturn is to short the Swedish Kroner or SEK.

THE SWEDISH KRONER'S DIRECTION AGAINST OTHER CURRENCIES

Long the EUR/SEK during potential market downturns

Long the USD/SEK during potential market downturns

Question: Why do these trades work out in such a way when the market is expected to go down?

Answer: The SEK against the USD and EUR goes down because the SEK follows market sentiment. As the world's traders feel that the market has too much risk built into it, they usually take steps to reduce their risk, hence a reduction in risk sentiment. The SEK follows this up and down, and performs remarkably in tandem with the European and U.S. market indexes.

Question: What if the market was expected to go up?

Answer: If the market was expected to move in the other direction and gain in value, then the opposite of the FX trades would be entered into, because the SEK moves with market risk sentiment. This is the same with the higher-yielding currencies such as the AUD, NZD, CAD, and NOK against the lower-yielding currencies: The lower-yielding currencies will be viewed as not offering enough return, while the high-yielding currencies will be thought to offer good risk/reward payoffs.

Other Trades to Consider

When the market is seen to be moving or will move in a downward or upward fashion, there is of course the potential for shorting or going long the traditional asset classes such as stock and futures.

▼ POTENTIAL TRADES FOR MARKET MOVEMENT

Market Moving UP	Market Moving DOWN
Long Index ETFs	Short Index ETFs
Long Bull 2x and 3x S&P 500 ETFs	Long Bear 2x and 3x S&P 500 ETFs
Long Bull 2x and 3x ETFs of Financial Stocks	Long Bear Financial 2x and 3x ETFs
Long Bull Dow 30 ETFs	Long Bear Dow 30 ETFs
Long Small Cap Stocks	Short Small Cap Stocks
Long Emerging Market ETFs	Short Emerging Market ETFs
Long E-Mini Index Futures	Short E-Mini Index Futures
Short VIX (Market Anxiety) Futures	Long VIX (Market Anxiety) Futures

There is a complete listing of day tradable ETFs listed by sector on Bloomberg's website: *www.bloomberg.com/markets/etfs.*

Here you will find the listing of some of the world's ETFs that have the most day trading possibilities. What you are looking for is volume in the number of shares bought and sold every day and the percentage movements. Two or 3 percent every day is a good place to start, as you can use leverage to get the percentage movement up to around 4–6 percent daily. Also, you can track the website and see how the bear and bull 2x and 3x basket ETFs are performing against the indexes of the underlying stocks. After studying for a week or two, you might decide that a 2x or a 3x bull ETF is perfect for you to trade, and you can go from there.

APPENDIX D

Financial Publications

There are dozens of publications that can be very helpful to investors and traders alike. These financially oriented newspapers, magazines, and newsletters offer valuable insights about the markets, including stock tips, mutual fund rankings, and in-depth articles with a more educational angle. Publications can be a good place to get investing and trading ideas, but you must still do your own research and analysis and make any investing or trading decisions.

The Wall Street Journal

Published by Dow Jones and Company, the *Wall Street Journal* is a leading global newspaper with a focus on business. Founded in 1889, the newspaper has grown to a worldwide daily circulation of more than 2 million readers. In 1994, Dow Jones introduced the *Wall Street Journal Special Editions*, special sections written in local languages that are featured in more than thirty leading national newspapers worldwide. The *Wall Street Journal Americas*, published in Spanish and Portuguese, is included in approximately twenty leading Latin American newspapers.
800-568-7625
www.wallstreetjournal.com

Barron's

Barron's is also known as the *Dow Jones Business* and *Financial Weekly*. With its first edition published in 1921, *Barron's* offers its readers news reports and analyses on financial markets worldwide. Investors will also find a wealth of tips regarding investment techniques.
800-975-8620
www.barrons.com

Investor's Business Daily

Founded in 1984, *Investor's Business Daily* is a newspaper focusing on business, financial, economic, and national news. The publication places a strong emphasis on offering its readers timely information on stock market and stock market–related issues. The front page of each issue provides a

brief overview of the most important business news of the day. It's published five days a week, Monday through Friday.
800-459-6706
www.investors.com

Forbes

Forbes magazine is a biweekly business magazine for "those who run business today—or aspire to." Each issue contains stories on companies, management strategies, global trends, technology, taxes, law, capital markets, and investments.
800-888-9896
www.forbesmagazine.com

Money

Money is a monthly personal finance magazine from Time-Warner publications, covering such topics as family finances, investment careers, taxes, and insurance. Each issue includes tips, advice, and strategies for smart investing. The magazine also features other related matters like finding cheap flights, buying a home, and preparing for tax season. It also offers a substantive annual mutual fund guide.
800-633-9970
http://money.cnn.com

BusinessWeek

This weekly publication comes jam-packed with comprehensive coverage of both the U.S. and global business scene. From the economy to politics to how both impact stock prices, *BusinessWeek* provides in-depth market analysis and incisive investigative reporting.
888-878-5151
www.businessweek.com

Fortune

Every month, *Fortune* magazine, a Time-Warner publication, offers analysis of the business marketplace. The publication's annual ranking of the top 500 American companies is one of its most widely read features. *Fortune* has been covering business and business-related topics since its origins in 1930.
800-621-8000
www.fortune.com

Smart Money

Smart Money, a monthly personal finance magazine, offers readers ideas for investing, spending, and saving. The publication also covers automotive, technology, and lifestyle subjects, including upscale travel, footwear, fine wine, and music.
800-444-4204
www.smartmoney.com

Kiplinger's Personal Finance

One of the most respected names in financial publications, *Kiplinger's* offers investing ideas, updates on companies, insider interviews with top financial experts and fund managers, and very detailed listings of the best-performing mutual funds in a wide range of categories.
800-544-0155
www.kiplinger.com

ValueLine Investment Survey

A weekly publication available at most libraries and through subscription, it offers ratings, reports, opinions, and analysis on about 130 stocks in seven or eight industries on a weekly basis. Approximately 1,700 stocks in about ninety-four industries are covered every thirteen weeks. CD-ROM subscribers can also purchase an expanded version containing reviews of 5,000 stocks.
800-634-3583
www.valueline.com

INDEX

A

B

C

D

E

F

G

H

I

J

L

M

N

O

P

Q

R

S

T

U

V

W

Z

We Have

EVERYTHING®

on Anything!

With more than 19 million copies sold, the Everything® series has become one of America's favorite resources for solving problems, learning new skills, and organizing lives. Our brand is not only recognizable—it's also welcomed.

The series is a hand-in-hand partner for people who are ready to tackle new subjects—like you!

For more information on the Everything® series, please visit *www.adamsmedia.com*

The Everything® list spans a wide range of subjects, with more than 500 titles covering 25 different categories:

Business
Careers
Children's Storybooks
Computers
Cooking
Crafts and Hobbies
Education/Schools
Games and Puzzles
Health
History
Home Improvement
Everything Kids
Languages
Music
New Age
Parenting
Personal Finance
Pets
Reference
Religion
Self-Help
Sports & Fitness
Travel
Wedding
Writing